THE
Steel City
GARDEN

creating a one-of-a-kind garden in black and gold

THE
Steel City
GARDEN

creating a one-of-a-kind garden in black and gold

DOUG OSTER
author of *Tomatoes Garlic Basil*

st. lynn's
press

PITTSBURGH

The Steel City Garden
Creating a One-of-a-Kind Garden in Black and Gold

Copyright © 2013 by Doug Oster

ISBN-13: 978-0-9855622-3-6

Library of Congress Control Number: 2013941485
CIP information available upon request

First Edition, 2013

St. Lynn's Press . POB 18680 . Pittsburgh, PA 15236
412.466.0790 . www.stlynnspress.com

Book design—Holly Rosborough
Editor—Catherine Dees
Editorial interns—Allison Keene, Claire Stetzer

Kind permission given by Greenprints to reprint the story on page 78;
Story Author: Kathy Chapman • Story Artist: Matt Collins

Photo credits:
All photos are by the author, with the exception of the following:
Baker Creek Heirloom Seed Co., pages 124, 125, 126, 127, 129, 133, 134, 139
Paul Kelly, pages xii (middle), 23, 110, 128, 142 (middle), 158 (lower left)
Holly Rosborough, pages xii (bottom), 17 (top), 21, 30 (left), 77, 101, 131, 135, 137, 138
Carson Elder, pages 111, 112
Pam Panchak, author photo, page 164
stock images, pages 65, 73, 91 (mid. left), 110, 115, 117, 123 (bottom), 129 (bottom), 149

Printed in Canada on certified FSC recycled paper using soy-based inks

This title and all of St. Lynn's Press books may be purchased for educational, business, or sales promotional use. For information please write:
Special Markets Department . St. Lynn's Press . POB 18680 . Pittsburgh, PA 15236

10 9 8 7 6 5 4 3 2 1

To Cindy, Tim, Matt and Stephanie.

I'm always happiest when I'm with you.

TABLE OF CONTENTS

INTRODUCTION

The main goal in creating any garden is to have fun, and that's what this book is all about.

A Steel City Garden can be a tribute to a city, a way of life, your favorite sports teams – or just be a beautiful place to sit and enjoy. Whether it contains trees, shrubs, bulbs, veggies or flowers, a garden of black and gold can easily be created with some planning, compost and a little bit of work (although most gardeners call it therapy).

This book isn't just a list of black and gold plants; it shows you how to grow each and every one of these varieties. It also shows you how to get the green thumb you've always wanted…and do it organically.

It's a friendly guide to planting and maintaining your garden without having to reach for chemicals. The simple organic principles will not only give you your best garden ever, it will make it a welcome place for butterflies, bees and other pollinators. Goldfinches, swallowtail butterflies and honeybees are black and gold garden helpers, making our job in the garden easier. Removing chemicals from the gardening equation will also let the good bugs thrive in their relentless search to eat the bad bugs. Most importantly, it will make your garden a safe space for you, your friends, family and pets.

The varieties in this book just scratch the surface of the many black and gold plants available from nurseries, garden centers and online catalogs. I'm often asked, "What should I plant?" and I'm happy to tell you my favorites. In this book I write about the importance of daffodils and orange crocus in my garden. Both have a deep connection to my family; seeing them bloom reminds me of the people I love. Finding plants that speak to you in this way can make your garden all the more special. I encourage you to experiment and find plants that mean something to you.

The plants used in creating a Steel City Garden are only limited by your imagination. One of the thrills of gardening is the hunt for plants that work perfectly in your garden.

A brief history of Pittsburgh's black and gold

Do you know how black and gold became the colors for Pittsburgh? It goes back to the creation of a city seal in the 1800s. The design came from William Pitt's family coat of arms: a black shield decorated with three gold coins and topped with a gold crown. The city was later named for Pitt, who had been a prime minister of Great Britain. When a city flag was created, it repeated the colors.

Through the years, the colors also came to represent the steel industry and the two main ingredients used to create the metal: coal (black) and iron ore (gold).

Eventually, the colors became part of every major sports team in Pittsburgh.

What's inside

The plants I've selected are grouped by type: flowers; trees, shrubs and foliage; fruits and veggies. First up in each group, you'll see the gold plants (including yellows). Next, the blacks (yes, there are lots of them out there, even a black tulip), and then the combination plants that are both gold and black. You'll also find a complete index at the back of the book, cross-referenced with common and botanical names.

A Steel City Garden wouldn't be complete without a little fun and whimsy, so I've included a bevy of black and gold garden ornaments, a few nice garden tools, and a couple of black and gold pollinators you'll want to invite in.

And then there are the stories: I pay visits to three very special Steel City Gardens and introduce you to the people who created them.

I hope you find inspiration in these pages. A Steel City Garden is what you want it to be: it can be acres or it can be one pot filled with your favorite colors. The most important thing about creating a garden is to make it special for you and everyone who visits.

Have fun!

Doug

FLOWERS

BEGONIA
many cultivars

- Annual bedding plant
- Part sun to full shade

 Tip Some begonias grow from tubers. They can be stored in vermiculite over the winter and replanted in the spring.

Begonias are a great shade-loving plant that will thrive all season long. There are many yellow varieties and they all grow well in containers or in beds. Spend time at the nursery to find the ideal variety for your black and gold garden.

Most begonias grow anywhere from six to twelve inches high, and the same wide. Feed the plants once a week or every other week with an organic liquid fertilizer. Also, it's fun to take cuttings of plants and grow them indoors during the off-season. They will thrive on the windowsill and be garden-ready in the spring.

WHERE IT WORKS BEST

Morning sun and afternoon shade are perfect for begonias. Make sure they are growing in rich garden soil amended with compost, and keep the plants watered when rain is scarce.

PESTS AND DISEASES

Aphids, spider mites, caterpillars and fungal issues can affect begonias.

Aphids and spider mites: Control with insecticidal soap or horticultural oil.

Caterpillars: Control with Captain Jack's Dead Bugbrew.

Fungal issues: Prevent by applying a good organic fungicide.

PLANT PARTNERS

Black pansies

✿ Annual bedding plant, perennial in zones 8–10

✿ Full sun to part sun, best in full

 Tip Even though the plant is self cleaning and doesn't need deadheading, some gardeners like to shear off the flowers when they get a little tired, for a flush of new blooms.

This native plant is carefree, beautiful and drought resistant. Like many natives, it will keep pumping out the blooms all season without deadheading.

Pretty yellow flowers over fern-like foliage get about a foot tall and will spread another foot around. There are lots of other cultivars to experiment with if 'Solaire Yellow' cannot be found.

Easy to grow for showy yellow flowers all season long, bidens is a great pollinator plant, too.

This is one of the easiest plants to find at local nurseries and it pairs with many black annuals easily. When the sun is out, sit back and watch as the good bugs are drawn to its bright-colored flowers.

WHERE IT WORKS BEST

Bring on the heat for bidens, as it loves full sun and only needs to be watered about once a week when rain is scarce. The plant will thrive in a variety of conditions and enjoys well-drained soil.

When grown in good compost or a good planting mix in containers, bidens will do well all season long and will be covered in pretty yellow flowers.

PESTS AND DISEASES

If fungal issues arise, treat with an organic fungicide.

PLANT PARTNERS

Black petunias

BLANKET FLOWER
Gaillardia x *grandiflora* 'Gallo Yellow'

- ❀ Perennial for zones 4-9 and annual varieties
- ❀ Full sun to part sun

Tip Birds will enjoy the flowers' seeds if they are left on the plant at the end of the season.

There aren't many plants tougher than gaillardia, and there are many yellow varieties that will work in the Steel City Garden. 'Gallo Yellow' blanket flower is a wonderful, long-blooming perennial with bright yellow flowers that attract bees, butterflies and hummingbirds. A mass planting of these yellow flowers will make a spectacular show in the front of a sunny border.

Gaillardia grows a foot tall and wide and will benefit from a good layer of mulch. Blanket flower can take drought, but it will need water at some point. Water early in the morning and soak the base of the plant. Since it has such a long bloom time, gaillardia is great for containers, too.

WHERE IT WORKS BEST

Gaillardia is a sun lover that will grow in a wide variety of soils. It will benefit from a planting area with well-drained soil improved with organic matter like compost. Deadheading will make the plant bloom throughout most of the summer.

PESTS AND DISEASES

Aphids and various beetles and caterpillars will affect blanket flower. Also, fungal disease can sometimes trouble the plant.

Aphids: Control with insecticidal soap or horticultural oil.

Beetles and caterpillars: Captain Jack's Dead Bugbrew will work on any chewing pest. It's organic and safe for the good bugs (which don't chew).

Fungal issues: Clear them up with a good organic fungicide.

PLANT PARTNERS

Black mondo grass, ornamental elderberry and black pansies

CORYDALIS
Corydalis lutea

✿ Perennial plant for zones 3-9

✿ Part shade to full sun

🌼🌼 *Tip* Dig up extra seedlings and share them with gardening friends. They will smile and think of you when they bloom.

There's no doubt about it, corydalis lutea is my favorite perennial. I knew I was in good company when I saw corydalis blooming at the base of Windsor Castle in England.

Most perennials will bloom for only a month or two, tops; this one starts blooming in the spring and continues through frost. To have a plant come back each season with such a long flowering period makes life in the garden a dream. This is the plant that makes my garden look like someone is actually working in there.

Corydalis produces lots of one-inch, cheery little yellow flowers over greenish-gray foliage about two feet tall and a little wider. The plant thrives in dry shade, but will grow anywhere. After a couple of seasons the plant will form a nice colony by throwing seeds around the garden. Corydalis is both deer and drought resistant, and I've seen it thrive without rain for weeks on end. In my opinion, it's the perfect plant.

WHERE IT WORKS BEST

Corydalis lutea is one of the most flexible plants in the garden. Since it spreads through seed instead of underground runners, it's not invasive and pulls out easily if it shows up in an unwanted spot. In my garden, it's allowed to ramble at will. It will sprout just about anywhere and I'm always glad to see it come up in my containers. It's ideal for pots, due to its long bloom time.

PESTS AND DISEASES

No serious pests or diseases.

PLANT PARTNERS

Black sweet potato vine, bugbane and cornflower

- Hardy bulb for zones 3-8
- Full sun to part sun

 Tip Fill the lawn with crocus in the fall and they will make a spectacular display the next spring. Just be sure not to cut the grass until the greens have faded back into the bulb. It will make for a beautiful garden and is such a great excuse not to cut the grass.

Sometimes a plant can transcend the boundaries of the garden and capture our hearts. My mother wasn't really into gardening, but she had a little patch of orange crocus growing by the front door. Every spring, I would run home from school to be welcomed by those crocuses.

They signal the change in the seasons and the passage of time, which is why they had such an emotional effect on me the last day I was in that house. I was doing okay until I turned around and saw those little crocus flowers staring at me.

I plant 'Golden Yellow,' 'Yellow Mammoth' and others every fall, and when they bloom in the spring, I'm reminded of those wonderful days growing up in the country.

A crocus only blooms for a few weeks, but it flowers right when we need it, first thing in the spring. These beautiful flowers are easy to grow and will last a lifetime when happy.

WHERE IT WORKS BEST

It's pretty easy to find a spot with full sun for crocus bulbs, as the trees will not have leafed out yet. The key to long life in most bulbs is to plant them where they can dry out in the summer. Be warned that you shouldn't plant impatiens over spring bulbs. All the water used to keep the impatiens alive will drown the bulbs.

PESTS AND DISEASES

Chipmunks will find the bulbs after they bloom and dig them out for a tasty treat. Try adding some sharp gravel in the planting hole to dissuade the cute pests.

PLANT PARTNERS

Dark-colored crocus

- Perennial for zones 3-9
- Full sun to part sun

Tip Plant daffodils in informal drifts, not as a line of soldiers. Throw the bulbs out on the ground and plant them where they land.

Do yourself a favor and plant some daffodils this fall. And don't just think they're all yellow trumpets; there's a wide variety of sizes and flower shapes.

My connection with daffodils goes back to 1967, when I was visiting my grandparents' graves at Lake View Cemetery in Cleveland. Daffodil Hill there was in full bloom and I was profoundly affected by the flowers. It is a sight to see.

When I moved to Pittsburgh, I decided to make my own Daffodil Hill by adding 1,000 bulbs a year. I recommend using a bulb auger for planting. It's a giant drill bit attached to a power drill, and it makes planting bulbs fun again. The old-fashioned hand planter is cruel and unusual punishment for gardeners!

I'm a sucker for double daffodils like 'Tahiti's. Search for varieties that you can fall in love with. You can buy mixed daffodils, too, a great way to add lots of bulbs on the cheap.

WHERE IT WORKS BEST

There are lots of areas where daffodils will thrive. They love full sun, but can be planted along drip lines of deciduous trees. Since the trees are bare when the daffs bloom, everything works out. The bulbs also get what they want when the tree is filled with foliage: a nice dry spot for the summer. It's the key to making most bulbs thrive.

PESTS AND DISEASES

Mostly pest and disease free

PLANT PARTNERS

Pansies, corydalis and violas

DAYLILY
Hemerocallis, many cultivars

- Perennial plant, zones 1-11 depending on variety
- Full sun to part sun

Tip Daylily buds are edible and are considered a delicacy in the kitchen.

Although every season sees many new daylily cultivars introduced, we're most interested in the yellow and gold varieties.

Sometimes called the perfect perennial, daylilies are one of those plants that will thrive regardless of the soil and light. Daylilies also partner well with daffodils; as the spring bulbs fade and the foliage becomes unsightly, the emerging daylily foliage will cover the brown daffodil leaves.

Of the many types of daylilies found in the garden, 'Stella de Oro' has probably become the most planted daylily in the world. It's a biannual re-bloomer, flowering from early summer until the start of winter. 'Fragrant Returns' has creamy yellow flowers that are lightly ruffled in appearance. 'Rumbleseat Romance' has fragrant yellow petals around a dark burgundy center. This final example is as close as we can get to black and gold.

WHERE IT WORKS BEST

Daylilies will bloom just about anywhere, but they will thrive in good soil and full sun. Don't skimp on the compost – the beds should be rich loam. Be sure to divide the plants every three to five years to keep them happy; rebloomers should be divided every two years, as new growth supports the rebloom. When the foliage starts to look terrible after blooming, cut it to the ground so it can regrow fresh green leaves.

PESTS AND DISEASES

Daylilies are mostly pest and disease free. However, thrips can attack the bud and distort the flower when it blooms, and you might see aphids and spider mites, as well.

Thrips and aphids and spider mites: Spray the plant with insecticidal soap or horticultural oil. Both are organic controls that need to cover the insect to be effective.

PLANT PARTNERS

Black-eyed Susans, bidens, black mondo grass, daffodils

✿ Perennial
plant for
zones 2-9

✿ Full sun to
part sun

 Tip Fernleaf yarrow self-sows readily; deadhead the plant if you don't want seedlings.

Fernleaf yarrow is an easy plant to grow. Its foliage is both ferny and fragrant. The clusters of bright yellow flowers can be as large as five inches across on stems three to four feet tall. Butterflies can't resist the flowers.

Fernleaf yarrow is a great multi-purpose plant. It is drought resistant and doesn't appeal to deer. It provides a dramatic yellow accent for the garden, it gives lots of cut blooms for the vase, and the flowers are a favorite for drying.

It's wonderful used in the back of a sunny border and will bloom for a long time if you give it a little extra water when needed. The bright yellow flowers seemingly glow in the sunlight.

WHERE IT WORKS BEST

Fernleaf yarrow is a full sun plant that likes average garden soil. The plant might need staking, especially if it's in a place in the garden that gets some shade. The tall yellow flowers look beautiful in a mass planting. Cut the flowers as they fade to keep the plant blooming.

PESTS AND DISEASES

Aphids, mealybugs and thrips are the three worst pests for this plant. Fungal issues can affect it, too.

Aphids, mealybugs and thrips: Control with insecticidal soap or horticultural oil. Be sure to coat the insects and the undersides of the leaves with the soap or oil.

Fungal issues: Use an organic fungicide.

PLANT PARTNERS

None needed.

GAZANIA
Gazania, many cultivars

- Annual bedding plant, tropical perennial for zones 8-10
- Full sun

 Tip All parts of the plant are poisonous to humans and pets, so be careful.

Gazania is a tough plant, usually grown as an annual. It loves full sun and dry soil and is a great choice for rocky beds. The petals can be both black and gold, but there are many different varieties, even one that is pure yellow. The flowers close at night or during gray days, opening again as soon as the sunlight hits them. Some gardeners pass on planting gazanias for this reason, but that's one of the things I love most about them. Some days, they welcome you to the garden with their brilliant colored blooms; other days, it's the pointed petals, closed and waiting. Either way, they are beautiful in my mind.

They bloom best with vigilant deadheading. Removing the spent flowers will force the plant to make more flowers for bees and butterflies to visit all summer long.

WHERE IT WORKS BEST

Grow gazanias in full sun; it's the only place where they will be happy. The plants thrive in good garden soil that's filled with compost or another organic soil amendment. Water as needed, but don't overdo it, because gazanias are drought resistant.

PESTS AND DISEASES

Gazanias are pretty much pest and disease free, but can be troubled by slugs, aphids, thrips, whiteflies and fungal issues.

Slugs: Use the organic bait Sluggo.

Aphids, thrips, whiteflies: Control with insecticidal soap or horticultural oil.

Fungal issues: Clear them up with a good organic fungicide.

PLANT PARTNERS

Black or yellow annuals such as **pansies**, and the perennial, black mondo grass

HELIOPSIS
Heliopsis helianthoides 'Tuscan Sun'

- ❀ Perennial plant for zones 3-9
- ❀ Full sun to part sun

 Tip Some varieties self-sow like crazy. If the seedlings are not wanted, deadhead the flowers as soon as they have finished blooming. The foliage has been used for centuries in various folk remedies.

'Tuscan Sun,' pictured here, is one of the smallest members of the genus *Heliopsis*, reaching only about 20 inches tall. It's filled with pretty, yellow-orange, daisy-like flowers that look great in floral arrangements or in the garden.

Heliopsis is a close relative of Helianthus, the true sunflower, and is easy to grow in decent garden soil. Pinch it back early in the season to encourage branching, and deadhead often to keep the plant flowering longer.

When happy, 'Tuscan Sun' will flower from June until September. A mass planting of this variety is a treat in the summer garden. You might also want to try 'Ballerina,' which is taller and has semi-double flowers.

WHERE IT WORKS BEST

Heliopsis loves full sun and a soil rich in organic matter. It's drought resistant, but it benefits from regular watering when rain is scarce.

PESTS AND DISEASES

Heliopsis in general is mostly pest and disease free. 'Tuscan Sun' is bred for disease resistance and is said to fight off powdery mildew, but pests such as aphids can get after the plant.

Aphids: Spray the plant with insecticidal soap or horticultural oil.

PLANT PARTNERS

None needed.

IRIS

Iris, **many species and cultivars**

- Perennial plant for zones 3-10, often planted from rhizomes
- Full sun to part sun

 Tip Irises are one of the only plants that are best divided in midsummer (every three to four years).

The iris is a beautiful flower that comes in various forms. The name originates from the Greek word for rainbow, for its many colors. Some are yellow, others are nearly black and a few are both...perfect for a Steel City Garden. As the stars of the early summer garden, irises play an important role in the perennial border. Put a few cut flowers in a container with some shallow water for a great indoor show, too.

The yellow iris pictured here is an unknown cultivar photographed in a friend's garden. The blooms were only eight inches tall, but they attracted visitors with their electrifying color.

Choose an overcast day and improve the soil in the planting hole before dividing; you want to have the rhizome out of the soil for the shortest time possible. Bury only half of the rhizome below ground.

WHERE IT WORKS BEST

Irises bloom best in full sun with lots of water. Don't overdo it, but give them a good soaking once a week if rain is hard to come by. Irises shouldn't be mulched, since rhizomes are prone to rotting if left under moist mulch. Be sure to remove the seedpods after blooming to prevent seedlings from choking out the mother plants.

PESTS AND DISEASES

Slugs are the main pest for the iris since they both thrive in the same spot.

Slugs: Control with organic baits like Sluggo, handpick or trap with stale beer.

PLANT PARTNERS

None needed.

LAMIUM (Deadnettle, Yellow Archangel)

Lamium galeobdolon 'Hermann's Pride'

- Perennial for zones 4-8
- Full sun to part sun

 Tip Bumblebees can't resist the flowers. Get down on the ground and watch them work the pretty yellow blooms.

'Hermann's Pride' is one of my favorite plants in the garden. The foliage is streaked green and white, with yellow tubular flowers that start to appear in early summer. The leaves become even brighter when grown in the shade. It's absolutely stunning in the garden as a mass planting.

'Hermann's Pride' forms a nice shape after only a few short seasons and will keep returning year after year. The foliage of this perennial puts on a beautiful show, but the lovely flowers are icing on the cake. It's also deer resistant and attracts butterflies.

WHERE IT WORKS BEST

Be careful, 'Hermann's Pride' can become invasive if it is grown where it's too happy. Don't be too generous with water, because too much can cause problems. It loves part sun and will even thrive in dry shade. Like most plants, this one can cover some ground when given a little water and compost. Since it's a slow to medium grower, though, it will take a while.

PESTS AND DISEASES

Downy mildew, leaf spot and slugs and snails can bother lamium.

Downy mildew and leaf spot: Control with organic fungicides. Before signs appear, apply Cornell mixture: 1 gal. water, 1 T baking soda, 1 T horticultural oil, a drop or two of unscented dishwashing liquid.

Slugs and snails: Control with organic baits like Sluggo, trap with stale beer, or handpick.

PLANT PARTNERS

Cornflower and black sweet potato vine

LANTANA
Lantana camara 'Lucky Yellow'

❀ Annual bedding plant, perennial in the Deep South

❀ Full sun, part sun

 Tip All parts of the plant, including seeds, are poisonous – and toxic to dogs and cats. So be careful.

Florida gardeners might think we're crazy up north for growing lantana. To them it's a weed, but to us it's a wonderful addition to the garden. It's also a common perennial in the warm climates in the West.

This easygoing plant will grow just about anywhere and doesn't need any special requirements. I love it in hanging baskets, as it will trail over the edges for close inspection from visitors. Versatile and hardy, lantana also has built-in defense mechanisms. It's deer resistant and survives well in drought, making it simple to care for.

'Lucky Yellow' and other plants from the same series are pretty easy to find, but there are plenty of other yellow cultivars out there that would look wonderful in your Steel City Garden. Bees and butterflies are drawn to the flowers. There's nothing like sitting in the garden and watching as the pollinators dance around the blooms. Hummingbirds also enjoy the flowers, just like you'll enjoy their visits.

WHERE IT WORKS BEST

All you need is sun, but don't worry if you can't place it perfectly. It's not fussy about the soil and loves hot weather. This workhorse will pump out the blooms even in part sun. As you're searching for your ideal yellow lantana, keep in mind that most new cultivars shed their spent blooms. Don't forget, however, to deadhead in order to keep the plant looking its best.

PESTS AND DISEASES

Pretty much pest and disease free.

PLANT PARTNERS

Black coleus, black elephant ear and black bugbane

- Annual bedding plant
- Full sun to part sun

 Tip Deadheading will keep the plant flowering all summer.

There's just nothing like a wonderful, yellow marguerite daisy in the garden. There are plenty of different cultivars out there, most of which will grow two or three feet high and a foot or so wide, and are deer resistant.

Their classic beauty also works in containers, where new cultivars are designed to be the thriller in the center of the pot. These newer varieties do much better in the heat but still love cooler temperatures at night.

Gardeners in warmer climates need not avoid marguerite daisies, however. In climates where nighttime temperatures are over 70°F, gardeners can give their plants a haircut during the hottest months to get them to branch and form more flowers. When things cool down, the plants will start blooming again. Butterflies will flock to the blooms, as will your gardening friends.

WHERE IT WORKS BEST

The perfect condition for marguerite daisies is morning and early afternoon sun and late afternoon shade. Give them plenty of compost, water and organic fertilizer to keep them blooming strong all season.

PESTS AND DISEASES

The plants are mostly disease free, but they do contend with some pests: aphids, mealybugs, spider mites, thrips and caterpillars.

Aphids, mealybugs, spider mites, thrips: Control by spraying insecticidal soap or horticultural oil.

Caterpillars: Control with Captain Jack's Dead Bugbrew.

PLANT PARTNERS

Black bugbane, black sweet potato vine and cornflower

Tagetes erecta 'Inca Gold II'

- ❀ Annual bedding plant
- ❀ Full sun to part sun

Tip Keep pinching spent flowers and this marigold will reward you with blooms galore all season long.

Not every gardener embraces marigolds the way I do. I love how they look and I love how they smell. There are many yellow flowering marigold varieties available, but 'Inca Gold II' is the perfect color for our purposes.

This early blooming variety has sturdy stems and incredible three-inch, double golden flowers. The plant reaches a foot in height and about the same wide.

Marigolds are one of the easiest plants to start from seed. Six to eight weeks before the last frost of the season, sprinkle seeds onto a moist planting mix and lightly cover them with the same mix. Cover the flat with plastic and put it under good light. Once the seeds sprout, remove the plastic and keep the light within an inch of the plants.

Gradually allow the plants to get used to the outdoors, and plant them out in the garden after the danger of frost has passed.

WHERE IT WORKS BEST

Marigolds will grow just about anywhere, but they do best with plenty of sun. They enjoy good garden soil and, with a healthy dose of compost, will bloom from frost to frost.

PESTS AND DISEASES

Slugs, Japanese beetles and fungal disease can bother marigolds.

Slugs: They love marigold seedlings. Control with organic baits like Sluggo, trap with stale beer, or handpick.

Japanese beetles: Control with Captain Jack's Dead Bugbrew.

Fungal disease: An occasional problem when the weather is wet and humid. Use an organic fungicide.

PLANT PARTNERS

Cornflower, black sweet potato vine and bugbane

MELAMPODIUM
Melampodium paludosum 'Showstar'

- Annual bedding plant
- Full sun to part sun

 Tip As long as you don't overwater 'Showstar,' the plant will be happy all season long.

Here's a wonderful and underused annual garden plant, also known as golden medallion flower, star daisy or butter daisy. It's tough, beautiful, fast growing and drought resistant. This colorful annual spreads to about 16 inches, with dainty yellow flowers protruding about two feet above green foliage. Butterflies will enjoy the flowers and, with a little water and liquid organic fertilizer, the plant will flourish.

The plant self-sows freely, producing seedlings all over the garden – which can be a good thing. Save some seeds to trade or give away to friends.

'Showstar' is easy to grow from seed and should be sown indoors six to eight weeks before the last frost.

WHERE IT WORKS BEST

'Showstar' and other melampodiums do best in full sun. They will survive and bloom with a little shade, though. They love the heat, and as an added defense, are deer resistant.

PESTS AND DISEASES

Mostly pest and disease free.

PLANT PARTNERS

Black sweet potato vine and black mondo grass

MEXICAN SUNFLOWER

Tithonia rotundifolia 'Yellow Torch'

- Annual bedding plant
- Full sun, part sun

 Tip Let the plant go to seed at the end of the season to save the seeds for next season's garden.

Mexican sunflowers are making a comeback. This easy-to-grow annual is a late bloomer, and 'Yellow Torch' is the perfect color for a Black and Gold garden.

For years, I grew 'Torch,' a variety that blooms with orange flowers. Then I found 'Yellow Torch.' A mass planting of 'Yellow Torch,' with its cheerful yellow flowers, looks like a pool of sunshine. I was thrilled to see this version of Mexican sunflower in the Baker Creek Heirloom Seeds catalog. I've never seen it growing in another garden, but I'm sure that's going to change.

Anyone who visits my garden comments on the bright yellow flowers held six feet in the air. It's a giant plant with branches two to three feet wide, and it never fails to impress. Just like human visitors, humming birds and butterflies can't resist the blooms. I love to sit in the garden listening to the hummers as they establish territory and swoop down to feed.

WHERE IT WORKS BEST

Full sun is best, but tithonia will also bloom with part sun, and does not normally need staking. It will grow adequately in average garden soil, but a mulch of compost will make it into a small tree by the end of the season. Seeds can either be started indoors a few weeks before the last frost or direct seeded in the ground. I prefer to plant transplants, however, as the flowers arrive earlier. Deadhead the spent flowers to keep the plant pushing out blooms.

PESTS AND DISEASES

Slugs and snails can get after the seedlings when they're small, but the problem is nothing serious.

Slugs and snails: Control with organic baits like Sluggo, trap with stale beer, or handpick. Toads will eat lots of slugs, so encourage them to live in your garden.

PLANT PARTNERS

Elephant ear, black and gold petunias and cornflower

❀ **Annual bedding plant**

❀ **Full sun to part sun**

Tip Nasturtiums are edible and delicious. I love to feed them to garden visitors. Bite into a nasturtium and you're met with the subtle watercress flavor, followed by a sweet heat released by the center of the flower. They are great when sprinkled on salads or used as an edible garnish on other dishes.

Nasturtiums are easy annuals to grow. Usually, the seeds are direct sowed into the garden, after the danger of frost has passed. There are many yellow varieties that will work wonderfully in the Steel City Garden. Some varieties have variegated foliage, and most have roundish foliage that appears before the pretty flowers emerge. Nasturtiums are drought resistant, love the heat and attract butterflies to their blooms. There are both climbers and mounding varieties. I grow mostly the latter. I have accidentally sowed a climber or two that surprised me by working their way up the hook of a hanging basket and trailing out the sides.

The 'Alaska' series has beautiful, variegated foliage. 'Canary Creeper' has cool-looking fringed, yellow flowers. And 'Jewel of Africa' has yellow flowers on a vine that can grow four to five feet tall.

WHERE IT WORKS BEST

Full sun and average to poor soil is a great place for nasturtiums. Be warned: when planted in a spot where they are too happy, the plant will produce lots of foliage at the expense of the flowers. And those yellow flowers are what you want to see!

PESTS AND DISEASES

Nasturtiums are relatively care-free, but they can be plagued by aphids.

Aphids: Insecticidal soap or horticultural oil are both great organic controls for the pests. Be sure to coat the insects with the soap or oil; don't forget the undersides of the leaves.

PLANT PARTNERS

Black and gold petunias and black mondo grass

OSTEOSPERMUM (African Daisy)

Osteospermum, **many cultivars**

- ❀ Annual bedding plant
- ❀ Full sun to part sun

 Tip Deadheading will keep the plant flowering all summer.

Osteospermum? Who comes up with these names? It sounds like a whale with a back issue. I much prefer to call this lovely flower the African daisy but, really, the best way to identify plants is with their proper Latin names.

Though the plant comes in many colors, we're interested in the bright yellow varieties. They will light up the garden with their sunny color, and most will grow at least a foot tall. Some will even reach three feet.

Easy to grow and attractive to butterflies, the African daisy is especially popular in the Deep South (zones 10-11). Like most daisy-like plants, they give us great cut flowers to brighten up the home.

Osteospermum should also be considered for containers, where it will thrive as a thriller or a filler, depending on its height.

WHERE IT WORKS BEST

Ostespermum is best planted in full sun, if possible. It will bloom with part sun, but will be happiest out in the open. Plant African daisies in good garden soil and mulch them to keep the roots moist. They do best in cooler climates; blooms will slow in hot, humid weather.

PESTS AND DISEASES

African daisies are pretty much pest and disease free, but watch for aphids and fungal issues.

Aphids: Control with insecticidal soap or horticultural oil.

Fungal issues: They can arise in humid conditions; use an organic fungicide.

PLANT PARTNERS

Black elephant ear and black sweet potato vine

Primula, many cultivars

- Perennial for zones 3-8
- Full sun to part sun

Tip Primroses can be divided in the fall if care is taken to dig deeply and treat the tap root gingerly.

Primroses are one of the first perennials to bloom, sometimes as early as late winter. There are many different cultivars and flower forms of the primrose, but for our purposes we're looking at the yellow varieties. Most of the varieties are only a foot or so tall and are spectacular when planted in a mass. Primrose is a favorite in English gardens, which should tell you something about its preferred environment.

Many a gardener's first introduction to the plant is as a holiday houseplant gift. After it's finished blooming, it's transplanted into the garden and, hopefully, returns year after year.

Primroses are most often bought as plants from the nursery, but if you're adventurous, it's easy to start them from seed. Have fun with this perennial. When it finds a place where it's happy, it will thrive for many seasons, even decades. The plant is also deer resistant and can be grown at the edge of woodlands without protection.

WHERE IT WORKS BEST

The plants love cool, rainy weather and need fertile soil amended with compost. They do best during a mild winter. In hotter climates, they can be planted in the shade of a deciduous tree, so as the season progresses, the tree's leaves will return, giving the primrose plants protection from the hot summer sun. Provide plenty of water when rain is scarce.

PESTS AND DISEASES

Spider mites are the main enemy of primrose and can infest the plant. Fungal issues can also appear, since primroses are grown during cool, wet weather.

Spider mites: Control with insecticidal soap or horticultural oil.

Fungal issues: Treat the plants with an organic fungicide.

PLANT PARTNERS

Black pansies would be perfect planted with yellow primroses. Black crocuses poking through the primrose foliage would also make a great spring scene.

* Tropical plant, often grown as a houseplant, for zones 9-11
* Part sun to shade

Tip Shrimp plants can be propagated by taking cuttings.

Although it's often grown as a houseplant, the shrimp plant is great in the garden, too. In fact, it's also the perfect shade-loving container plant.

Shrimp plants grow to be one to two feet tall, and when grown where they are happy, will be covered with lovely yellow and white blooms. Interestingly, the yellow blooms are not actually flowers – they're bracts. But the tiny white flowers that grow from the bracts are true flowers. This yellow shrimp plant is one of the many cultivars that produce various colored bracts. It makes a stunning combination when grown with 'Black Dragon' coleus.

If grown on the windowsill during the winter, give it as much light as possible in a south-facing window. In hot, sunny, tropical climates, the plant can become a bushy, evergreen small shrub. When it's not blooming, pinch the tips of the shrimp plant to encourage branching and, in turn, more bracts.

WHERE IT WORKS BEST

Shrimp plants will grow in a variety of conditions, from full sun (with plenty of water) to shade. Morning sun and afternoon shade are perfect for the plant when grown outside. It's also an easy container plant. The soil should be fertile loam, and the plant needs regular watering. When the plant is indoors, however, don't overwater.

PESTS AND DISEASES

Shrimp plants are pretty free of pests and diseases. Sometimes spider mites will bother the plant, and it can be affected by fungal issues.

Spider mites: Spray the plant with insecticidal soap or horticultural oil several times over a few weeks. This organic control needs to come in contact with the pest to be effective.

Fungal issues: Use an organic fungicide like Serenade.

PLANT PARTNERS

'Black Dragon' coleus, black sweet potato vine and bugbane.

Annual
bedding
plant,
short-lived
perennial in
zones 8-10,
usually only
lasts a few
seasons

 Full sun

 Tip Strawflowers are easy to grow from seed. They should be started indoors about six to eight weeks before the last frost of the season.

S trawflowers come in many colors, but it's the yellow varieties we're most interested in. A yellow strawflower will make you smile, in addition to working well in the Steel City Garden.

The yellow, daisy-like flowers aren't actually flowers, but stiff, paper-like bracts. As a result, they make great dried arrangements and wreaths. The everlasting flowers can be cut before they fully open and hung upside down for a few days to completely dry out.

It's always nice to see them on the mantel during the winter months, a happy reminder of the warmth of the summer garden.

Depending on the variety, they will grow anywhere from eighteen inches to four feet tall.

WHERE IT WORKS BEST

Full sun and well-drained soil is what strawflowers need to thrive. They will still bloom with a little shade, but not as well as out in the open. Strawflowers are drought resistant and easy to grow — perfect for hot, dry beds.

PESTS AND DISEASES

These flowers are mostly pest and disease free. You might see some aphids, downy mildew or other fungal issues.

Aphids: They can be controlled with insecticidal soap or horticultural oil.

Downy mildew and other fungal issues: Prevent them by applying an organic fungicide.

PLANT PARTNERS

Black and gold petunias

- ✿ Annual bedding plant
- ✿ Full sun to part sun

Tip Keep the plant deadheaded for constant blooms. Water at the base when possible to avoid fungal diseases.

There are lots of yellow zinnias out there, with 'Profusion Yellow' being one of the stars. This stunning plant boasts two-inch flowers that make a spectacular addition to any garden. I can't have a vegetable garden without a row of zinnias. They brighten any place they're planted. This particular variety grows a little taller than a foot and, when happy, will reach 9 or 10 inches across.

Most gardeners probably plant them from flats, which is fine, but I prefer to direct sow them in the garden when possible. They always seem to do better for me that way and avoid powdery mildew.

Butterflies, hummingbirds and bees love zinnias. It's wonderful to sit close to the flowers and watch the variety of wildlife that visits the blooms. Just as this beautiful cultivar will brighten your garden, it will add beauty to your home as a long-lasting cut flower.

WHERE IT WORKS BEST

Zinnias love full sun and thrive in heat, but will flower with part sun. But the less sun, the more susceptible they are to powdery mildew. Plant zinnias in good garden soil amended with compost; a layer of mulch will keep the soil evenly moist and the plants growing strong. Zinnias are heavy feeders and will enjoy a regular dose of organic liquid fertilizer.

PESTS AND DISEASES

Zinnias are tough and usually pest free when they're growing strong. This variety is mildew resistant, but powdery mildew can still affect it. Aphids, whiteflies and spider mites can also cause potential problems.

Aphids, whiteflies and spider mites: Control them organically with insecticidal soap or horticultural oil.

Powdery mildew: Use organic fungicides or the Cornell mixture (see p. 25).

PLANT PARTNERS

Black sweet potato vine and cornflower

Solenostemon, many species and cultivars

❁ Annual
flower

❁ Part sun
to shade

 Tip It's easy to take cuttings of coleus to make more plants. Just cut some of the outer stems, dip them in Rootone and stick them in some slightly moistened planting mix. Cover the container with plastic to keep the humidity up, and store it in a shady spot. In a couple of weeks, remove the plastic and gently tug on the plants. If they resist, they have rooted and can be potted up to the next size container.

When I walked into the Sunken Garden room at Phipps Conservatory and Botanical Garden here in Pittsburgh, I was thrilled to see luminescent yellow shrimp plants behind a deep black coleus. The display was stunning, a perfect Steel City Garden combination.

Of all the dark red and purple coleus available, 'Black Dragon,' shown here with the shrimp plant, is one of the darkest I've ever seen. Since my house is surrounded by huge oak trees and the plant thrives in shade, I have grown lots of coleus. It can take some sun, though, but the more sun it gets, the more water it will need.

WHERE IT WORKS BEST

Coleus is best suited for shade or part sun. They make great container plants and they enjoy fertile soil. Many gardeners pinch off the flowers to keep the plants branching, but I love the look of the tiny flowers and have even had some plants reseed. Since coleus is a shade lover, bring in a few plants to grow on the windowsill for the off-season.

PESTS AND DISEASES

Coleus has few problems, but can be susceptible to mealybugs and fungal issues.

Mealybugs: Insecticidal soap or horticultural oil will take care of the mealybugs after a few applications. Be sure to coat the pest with the spray.

Fungal issues: Make sure coleus is planted in a well-drained area and has proper spacing for air circulation – necessary to prevent downy mildew (which can be fatal) and other fungal diseases.

PLANT PARTNERS

Begonias, pansies and shrimp plant

Centaurea montana 'Black Sprite'

❄ **Perennial for zones 3-8**

❄ **Full sun**

Tip Cut the plant back after flowering, to get fresh foliage.

Looking for a plant that's unique in the garden? Try 'Black Sprite' cornflower. It has amazing black, frilly flowers that play nicely against its silvery-gray, fuzzy foliage. The plant can reach two feet tall and about a foot wide.

Bees and butterflies love the flowers. The blooms make wonderful cut flowers and can also be dried. Plant a drift of three or five and watch these thistle-like flowers sway in the breeze when they bloom during the summer.

When we first start gardening, we're just glad when something lives. Once we get past that, we want to grow something different. 'Black Sprite' fits the bill. It's easy to grow and not fussy at all.

WHERE IT WORKS BEST

'Black Sprite' needs full sun to thrive. Don't try it anywhere else. Give it a good home in the form of well-drained, organic-rich soil, and don't overwater. The plant can be divided every two or three years to keep it vigorous.

PESTS AND DISEASES

Aphids, rust and powdery mildew will sometimes find cornflowers.

Aphids: Control with insecticidal soap or horticultural oil.

Rust and powdery mildew: Remove infected foliage as soon as it's seen, then treat with an organic fungicide.

PLANT PARTNERS

Any yellow flowers. Try a perennial like the beautiful yellow **'Klondyke' azalea** or annuals like marigolds and marguerite daisies.

Tulipa, many cultivars

- ❀ Hardy bulb for zones 3-8
- ❀ Full sun to part sun

Tip Be sure to deadhead tulips after they bloom. This allows the plant to put its energy into the bulb instead of seed-making.

Tulips aren't around very long each year in our gardens, but when you see them in bloom, there's nothing like them. They are the most wonderful spring cut flower.

For our purposes, black and yellow varieties are easily found in catalogs or at the nursery. For black, 'Queen of the Night,' pictured here, is a favorite of mine. 'Golden Parade' is the perfect gold variety for the black and gold garden, but many others will work, too.

Tulips are planted in the fall, 8 to 12 inches deep in good soil that's amended with compost. The trick is to make them come back every year, since they are short-lived for many gardeners. I find the 'Darwin' variety to be the most perennial. I tend to plant tulips every year, treating them like annuals. Some will continue blooming each spring for a decade, and others peter out in just a few short seasons.

WHERE IT WORKS BEST

Tulips like full sun, and they must be planted in well-drained soil in order to dry out through the summer. The better the drainage, the more perennial the tulips will be. Problem areas for some plants can be the perfect place for tulips; since they must dry out through the summer, tulips will thrive at the edges of the drip line of deciduous trees.

PESTS AND DISEASES

Tulips are fairly pest free. Some aphids or slugs might get after them, but both are easily controlled with organic methods.

Aphids: Control with insecticidal soap or horticultural oil.

Slugs: Control with organic baits like Sluggo, trap with stale beer, or handpick.

PLANT PARTNERS

Black and yellow tulips planted together will look spectacular.

Rudbeckia, many cultivars

- Perennial for zones 3-11
- Full sun

 Tip All parts of the plant are poisonous, and toxic to pets as well, so be careful.

The black-eyed Susan is the poster child for the Steel City Garden; that's why it's on the cover of the book.

Color-wise, it has everything for our purposes. These are hardy plants that will come back year after year, increasing the size of the clump annually.

The great thing about this plant is that the blooms last most of the summer. Black-eyed Susan works great as a mass planting. This is a tough perennial that should outlive the gardener. The flowers are wonderful in cut arrangements, too.

WHERE IT WORKS BEST

Black-eyed Susans enjoy full sun and good garden soil amended with plenty of compost. Mulch the plants with your favorite organic mulch.

PESTS AND DISEASES

The main things that bother black-eyed Susans are whitefly and, sometimes, fungal issues.

Whiteflies: They can be controlled with insecticidal soap or horticultural oil.

Fungal problems: A good organic fungicide should clear things up. If a stand of plants shows signs of fungal issues one season, apply the fungicide as the plant leafs out the next year.

PLANT PARTNERS

Bidens and marigolds

BLACK-EYED SUSAN VINE
Thunbergia alata

- ✿ Annual in most climates, perennial in zone 9 and higher
- ✿ Full sun, will bloom with a little shade, too

 Tip Deadheading will keep the plant flowering all summer.

The black-eyed Susan vine is tailor-made for a Steel City Garden, with its cheery black and gold flowers. The plant has deep yellow blossoms with black centers and thrives in good garden soil or compost. Black-eyed Susan vine is prolific and will cover a fence, arbor or even small children if they stand still long enough. The vines can reach eight feet or higher and make a bold statement in any garden.

There are many ways to use this frost-sensitive vine. It's a great container plant, but be sure to give it a pot big enough to let it run; three gallons or bigger if possible.

It's also a great garden plant, happy to ramble up and cover whatever support you decide to use. The plants are often sold in nurseries already well underway and ready to climb. Oftentimes they are offered with some climbing support already in place.

WHERE IT WORKS BEST

For a large-container grouping, try black-eyed Susan vine as the centerpiece and think about what might look great spilling over the edges to soften the edges of the pot (see Plant Partners). The plant can be started from seed eight weeks before the last frost. Gardeners with ample space and light, like a greenhouse, could start even earlier to produce a large, blooming plant ready to hit the ground running.

PESTS AND DISEASES

Whiteflies, spider mites and scale are the three pests that most frequently bother the black-eyed Susan vine.

Whiteflies and spider mites: Control with insecticidal soap or horticultural oil to cover the insect. Coat as much of the plant as possible, especially the undersides of the leaves.

Scale: Horticultural oil can work, but a dab of rubbing alcohol is probably a quicker solution.

PLANT PARTNERS

In a large-container planting: **Corydalis**, bidens ferulifolia 'Solaire Yellow' and petunias

Echinacea paradoxa 'Yellow Coneflower'

🌼 **Perennial wildflower for zones 3-9**

🌼 **Full sun to part sun**

 Tip If you have a problem area in full sun, that would be the perfect place for a mass of 'Yellow Coneflower.'

There are lots of yellow cultivars, but none tougher than 'Yellow Coneflower.' The only things left after a nuclear holocaust will be cockroaches, Keith Richards and 'Yellow Coneflower.'

Coneflowers are prairie plants; breeders have done amazing work with it, but sometimes there's no improving on what Mother Nature creates. Coneflowers are attractive to many pollinators, including butterflies, bees and wasps. Goldfinches love to feed on the seeds, too. The bright yellow petals of 'Yellow Coneflower' are complemented by gray/black centers. They will bloom for a long time, lasting for most of the summer.

This photo was taken on the green roof of the Center for Sustainable Landscapes on the campus of Phipps Conservatory and Botanical Gardens in Pittsburgh, one of the greenest buildings in the world. When necessary, the gardeners use saved rainwater for their plants.

WHERE IT WORKS BEST

This plant works best in large groupings. Don't spoil it. The plant needs average garden soil and a little water here and there. It's drought, deer and even flood resistant. When you combine its bright yellow color with its indestructible nature, you've got the perfect plant for the Steel City Garden.

PESTS AND DISEASES

No serious pest or disease problems plague 'Yellow Coneflower.'

PLANT PARTNERS

None needed.

- Annual tuber, can be saved indoors over the winter
- Full sun to part sun

 Tip After frost has blackened the foliage, dig out the tubers and put them in a dry place on newspaper. In a couple days put them in a box with moist vermiculite and store in a cool place that does not freeze. Check on the tubers once a month during the winter.

Add 'Mystic Illusion' to the list of perfect plants for the black and gold garden. It's right up there with black-eyed Susans and sunflowers for the perfect color combination.

Dark purple-black foliage sets off the star-shaped, bright yellow flowers on this easy-to-grow plant. 'Mystic Illusion' dahlias will get three feet tall and about two feet around. They would also be happy in a container.

Dahlias are a must in my garden and this one is a winner. I've talked to lots of gardeners who won't grow them because they don't want to save the tuber during the off season. Don't deny yourself the beauty of dahlias just because you don't want to fuss with the tuber. Just treat dahlias like an annual and let the tuber freeze during the winter. Gardeners in zone 6 and warmer might get a surprise the next spring, as the plant can survive, depending on the severity of the winter.

WHERE IT WORKS BEST

Dahlias are heat and sun lovers but will bloom even when conditions aren't ideal. The tuber can be either started in a pot a couple of weeks before the start of the season or planted directly in the garden when danger of frost has passed. Plants are also available from good garden centers and nurseries.

PESTS AND DISEASES

Dahlias have problems with aphids, thrips, caterpillars and fungal issues.

Aphids and thrips: Spray with insecticidal soap or horticultural oil.

Caterpillars: Control with Captain Jack's Deadbug Brew.

Fungal issues: If they appear, treat with an organic fungicide.

PLANT PARTNERS

None needed.

- Perennial plant for zones 4-8
- Full sun to part sun

 Tip Cut the plant back in early spring to encourage branching and more blooms.

Helenium is a type of perennial sunflower. Sometimes called sneezeweed or false sunflower, it has deep yellowish-orange flowers with dark chestnut centers, and it's a natural for a Steel City Garden.

Helenium should be in more gardens because it's so easy to grow and so beautiful. The three-foot-tall stems might need to be staked, though, especially if they're not in full sun. If you have some areas of part sun, you could check out shorter varieties, like 'Gilded Dwarf,' that will be happy with a little bit of shade.

Groupings of three to five plants placed throughout a border area will make quite a show in midsummer. And the bees, birds and butterflies will thank you.

WHERE IT WORKS BEST

Helenium needs full sun and good soil. Don't over-fertilize this plant, because that can lead to weak stems.

PESTS AND DISEASES

Helenium is mostly pest and disease free, but slugs can sometimes get to the foliage early in the season.

Slugs: Control with an organic bait like Sluggo, trap them with stale beer, or hand pick.

PLANT PARTNERS

None needed.

Orchid

 Part sun to full shade

 Tip There are thousands of types of orchids. Try growing a few, but be careful – it can be addictive.

If an outdoor garden isn't for you, an orchid on the windowsill or under lights might be something fun to try. They may have a scary growing reputation, but with a little research and a mildly green thumb, orchids can be pretty easy to care for.

These beautiful plants come in a variety of cultivars with multitudes of flower forms and growing habits, making them easy to fit into any lifestyle. One particular cultivar, the Aliceara Pacific Nova 'Pacific Heights' is ideal for a Steel City Garden display.

Don't let the name throw you; it may sound like it belongs on the West Coast, but I saw it blooming at Phipps Conservatory and Botanical Gardens in Pittsburgh and knew I had to photograph it for this book.

Consider giving this special plant a try in your Steel City Garden. Once you figure out the basic care, you'll be on a lifelong journey of discovery with this amazing plant.

WHERE IT WORKS BEST

Orchids are indoor plants, although they can enjoy the summer outdoors in a shady spot; they will love the humidity summer air brings.

I recommend growing orchids under lights, but be aware that most of these plants are killed by kindness. Too much water and fertilizer will make them give up the ghost. An orchid grower once told me to fertilize the plants weekly, weakly.

PESTS AND DISEASES

Aphids, mites and scale are probably the most common insect pests. Orchids are also plagued by a range of diseases, many of them fungal.

Aphids and mites: Control with insecticidal soap or horticultural oil.

Scale: Try horticultural oil and a dab of rubbing alcohol on the pest.

Fungal issues: An organic fungicide will be a start, but the diseases need to be controlled on a case-by-case basis.

PLANT PARTNERS

None needed.

- ✿ Half-hardy annual but sometimes perennial, depending on zone and severity of the winter
- ✿ Full sun to part shade

 Tip Replant pansies in the fall when tender annuals succumb to frost. As long as they are kept watered, pansies have a decent chance of overwintering in most climates. They will at least provide some color for the first few months of winter.

Pansies (and violas, a close relative) are the first flowers to plant as winter is winding down. Plant them in containers close to the house for protection. They can withstand freezing temperatures, lasting into midsummer. At that point, it usually gets too hot for them, and they can be replaced with bargain annuals from the nursery.

There are lots of varieties that bloom in black and gold. One of the prettiest is 'Victorian Yellow Picotee.' Although the blooms are smaller than most pansies, the petals are frilly around the edges and really stand out as a unique variety. 'Majestic Giants Yellow Blotch' offers a more typical flower type. The plant is prolific and will fill a container with beautiful black and gold blooms.

'Accord Black Beauty,' shown here, has small flowers of the darkest purple with yellow centers. Mixing all the varieties together would make a delightful Steel City Garden bed.

WHERE IT WORKS BEST

Pansies are cool weather plants that will enjoy full sun until things get hot. During the warmer months, they like morning sun and afternoon shade.

The plants need plenty of water and will benefit from a biweekly feeding of organic liquid fertilizer.

PESTS AND DISEASES

Pansies can be bothered by aphids, spider mites and slugs.

Aphids and spider mites: Control with insecticidal soap or horticultural oil.

Slugs: Control with organic baits like Sluggo, trap with stale beer, or hand pick.

PLANT PARTNERS

None needed when planting varieties that are black and gold. Yellow pansies can be grown with black pansies and vice versa.

PETUNIA
Petunia 'Phantom'

- Annual bedding plant
- Full sun to part sun, best in full

 Tip Most nurseries discount annuals about half way through the season. This is a great way to fill in beds that need color on the cheap. It's also a great time to refresh containers with the plants, which are usually sold in three-to four-inch pots.

I first saw 'Phantom' on a trip to Columbus, where the plant was being trialed at the Franklin Park Conservatory and Botanical Gardens.

This was years before I thought about writing this book, but even then I knew that black and gold gardeners would have to have this petunia.

These petunia blooms are striped yellow and black and will create a Steel City Garden all on their own. The plants are filled with these spectacular flowers and will grow to be about a foot tall and spread as wide.

The mounding upright habit works just about everywhere in the garden. 'Phantom' sheds its spent flowers pretty well, but like any petunia, will bloom better with some deadheading.

WHERE IT WORKS BEST

'Phantom' will grow anywhere other petunias would be happy. It's a great bedding plant and also works well in containers. Hanging baskets look especially dramatic, as the flowers will spill over the edges.

PESTS AND DISEASES

Petunias can suffer from a variety of pests, including aphids, spider mites and foliage-chewing caterpillars. They can also be affected by powdery mildew and other fungal diseases.

Aphids and spider mites: Control with insecticidal soap or horticultural oil.

Caterpillars: Try Captain Jack's Dead Bugbrew.

Powdery mildew and fungal diseases: Use organic fungicides.

PLANT PARTNERS

None needed. A flat of 'Phantom' will make an oasis of black and gold, although growing them beneath a black-eyed Susan vine would be pretty spectacular.

Annual
flower

 Full sun

 Tip Leave the large flowers on the stalks at the end of the season and let them dry. Birds will enjoy the seed all winter. You can remove the dried heads and store them. Through the winter, put out the heads for the birds. Or, harvest the seeds and fill feeders (saving some for the gardener).

There is something magical about a field of sunflowers. Have you ever driven past one? The giant yellow and black flowers simply can't be ignored.

Months after a tiny seed is dropped into fertile soil, the towering flower comes to fruition. There are many different types; some grow taller than 10 feet and others are perfect for a pot, reaching only 12 inches. Many varieties have one large flower on top of the stem, but others have a branching habit with many flowers.

Not all sunflowers will be both black and gold; many are pure yellow and some even have double flowers. And all of them attract butterflies, bees and birds to the garden. Sunflowers make a bold statement as cut flowers, filling a vase with their stunning colors.

Seeds are usually direct sowed in the garden, but you can buy transplants from a nursery. I like to plant them every few weeks, starting in the spring, to stagger the blooms.

WHERE IT WORKS BEST

Full sun is always best for sunflowers. Out in the open, the stems will grow thick and be able to support the large flower heads. Give the plants fertile, well-drained soil and water when rain is scarce. Sunflowers are easy to grow and put on a spectacular show all summer.

PESTS AND DISEASES

Rabbits, deer, squirrels and birds love to snack on the seeds and seedlings. The plants can also suffer from powdery mildew and other minor fungal issues.

Rabbits and deer: Physical barriers like plastic netting are the best ways to protect crops. Spray repellents are useful too.

Fungal issues: Use an organic fungicide like Serenade for fungus and the Cornell mixture (see p. 25) for powdery mildew.

PLANT PARTNERS

None needed.

🌼 **Perennial bulb for zones 2-9**

🌼 **Full sun to part sun**

 Tip Divide tiger lilies about every three seasons in the fall. When the plant is done blooming and the stems have started to decline, remove them to discourage diseases.

Summer is the season for lilies, when yellow tiger lilies are in their prime. They can be bought potted from a nursery, but it's most economical to start them from bulbs. The bulbs can often be found on sale in midsummer, and they are also sold for spring planting. It's fine to plant them either way as they form a large root mass similar to many other perennial plants.

Tiger lily bulbs can be planted just about any time of the season in soil that has been improved with compost. I like to plant them in the fall, when the temperatures are perfect for root growth. The bulb spends the end of the season underground, but not sleeping; it's preparing for next summer's blooms.

Yellow tiger lilies have the perfect color for our purposes. Plant them in drifts through a bed and don't forget to cut a few for a vase, to bring their beautiful color inside.

WHERE IT WORKS BEST

Full sun and average soil will keep tiger lilies happy, but adding compost will keep them happy for decades. The plants can reach six feet tall and sometimes need to be staked, especially when a little shade is involved. Stake them before they flop over, because once they take a dive, they never will look the same even when supported.

PESTS AND DISEASES

Tiger lilies are pest and disease resistant. Some beetles will attack the buds or plant, and the foliage can have some viral issues at times.

Beetles: Most chewing insects can be controlled with Captain Jack's Dead Bugbrew. It's organic and safe for the environment.

Viral diseases: Remove the foliage as it fades after blooming.

PLANT PARTNERS

None needed.

VIOLA
Viola, many cultivars

- Biennial, can act as a perennial in milder climates (even to zone 5 with the right winter)
- Full sun to part sun

 Tip Fall-planted violas can winter over if they are given a little protection. To make them last, be sure to water them before the first hard freeze of the season. They might even bloom again during a late winter thaw.

These low-growing plants can offer both black and gold blooms, and many have a delicate fragrance. Violas are among the first plants to be planted in the spring, and it's wonderful to have entryways filled with such cheery color so early in the season.

In my zone 6 garden, I plant my violas in containers in March. Keeping the pots close to the house helps protect them from the extreme cold. You can see that the viola in the photo is happily blooming through the snowfall in late winter. Feed them an organic, liquid fertilizer every other week to keep them blooming strong.

In the house, I like to float the flowers in a shallow dish of water – another fun way to enjoy the blooms. The edible petals also make great additions to salads. It's a wonderful surprise to serve them to guests, sharing in the delights of their subtle flavor.

WHERE IT WORKS BEST

These plants love cool weather and full sun, but will also thrive in part sun. Spring-planted violas will last for months, but they don't enjoy the summer heat. They can be kept alive with plenty of water, but I pull them out in the middle of summer and go find some discounted annuals from the nursery. Then, after the annuals succumb to frost, I re-plant the containers with violas.

PESTS AND DISEASES

Slugs, spider mites and aphids can affect the plant. Since violas are grown during cool, wet weather, fungal issues can appear.

Slugs, spider mites, aphids: Control with organic products.

Fungal issues: Treat the plants with an organic fungicide if problems occur.

PLANT PARTNERS

Black pansies

THE PERFECT COMBINATION
Euphorbia 'Breathless White', *Nemesia* 'Sunsatia Lemon'
Petunia 'Black Velvet'

- Annual bedding plants
- Full sun to part sun

 Tip Place containers in different areas of the garden to highlight black and gold plants.

This is an example of a perfect black and gold plant combination for containers. I found this grouping already planted together at Hahn Nursery in Ross Township, Pa. The combination is called Solar Eclipse, and was created by Schmidt Brothers growers in Swanson, Ohio.

Although this euphorbia's foliage doesn't strictly follow our black and gold theme, it looks great in the pot and makes a good backdrop for the two stars players. The 'Black Velvet' petunia is a great color for our purposes, while the 'Sunsatia Lemon' nemesia provides the gold to set off the black of the petunias.

You can do the same thing Schmidt Brothers did, by combining your favorites in a container. The possibilities are endless.

WHERE IT WORKS BEST

Set this container out in the full sun, keep it watered and fed and it will bloom all summer long.

PESTS AND DISEASES

With many flowers, watch for aphids, mealybugs, spider mites, thrips and fungal issues.

Aphids, mealybugs, spider mites and thrips: Control with insecticidal soap or horticultural oil.

Fungal issues: Treat with an organic fungicide.

PLANT PARTNERS

None needed.

A PITTSBURGH PETUNIA STORY

"Plant One for the Home Team" *by Kathy Chapman*

As Pat Stone and I sat at a Garden Writers of America awards banquet, congratulating each other on our recent wins, the conversation turned to The Steel City Garden. Pat is the creator of one of my all-time favorite garden publications, Greenprints. Instead of providing how-to's, Greenprints focuses on the human side of gardening – the therapy, enjoyment, frustration and beauty we receive from the garden.

As we chatted, he told me about a wonderful piece he published recently that's all about a black and gold garden. After reading Kathy Chapman's amazing story in the Winter 2012-2013 issue, I begged him to let me use it in this book. It perfectly expresses what the Steel City Garden means to fans of all things black and gold. Here is Kathy's story.

In my world, there are two seasons: gardening and hockey. I spend winter nights watching hockey on TV with a seed catalog on my lap. Spring is the time to plant and watch the National Hockey League playoffs. As summer finally drifts into fall, I welcome the harvest season and preseason games. And, to me, hockey means my beloved Pittsburgh Penguins.

I am a transplant to the Finger Lakes region of upstate New York, but my roots are deep in the Allegheny Mountains of Western Pennsylvania, just east of Pittsburgh. If you've ever met a former Western Pennsylvanian, you may have noticed our fierce (my husband, Ron, would say "cult-like") devotion to all things Pittsburgh.

My particular corner of New York State is beautiful, with its rolling hills and sparkling lakes. Vineyards and farms spread across the countryside like a patchwork quilt. Little waterfalls tumble through the gullies and glens. It's picturesque and pastoral, and I love it.

But it isn't Pittsburgh.

Pittsburgh is strong and manly, full of history and tradition. George Washington trod those steep hills. The Whiskey Rebellion started there. They eat things like chip-chop ham and drink Iron City beer, neither of which I cared much for when I lived there. But no matter; they're in Pittsburgh and I love them now. And Pittsburgh's colors are black and gold: like the Steelers' football uniforms, like the Pirates' baseball uniforms, and best of all, like my Pittsburgh Penguins' hockey jerseys.

And so it was that last May, halfway through the hockey playoffs, just as planting season was beginning, I visited my favorite garden store, looking for annuals for some containers. I wandered past the new-arrival display, with its million bells in shades of peach and geraniums in bright new colors. Something strange caught my eye: a black petunia with a yellow star. The tag called it Phantom. That seemed a fitting name for such a strangely colored flower. The price was high for a petunia, though, so I kept walking. Suddenly it hit me: That petunia was black and gold! It wasn't a Phantom petunia. It was a Pittsburgh petunia! I had to have some. Price was no object now.

I loaded my cart with my new favorite flower, along with yellow snapdragons and million bells to complement them. At the checkout, I couldn't contain my enthusiasm. "Look at these flowers!" I gushed to the cashier. "They're black and gold – just like the Pittsburgh

Penguins and the Steelers!" She looked at me as if I had petunias growing out of my ears. But she had to admit that could be a good marketing ploy for any other Pittsburgh fans who might come in.

Back home, I pulled in our driveway and shouted to Ron, "Guess what? I got some Pittsburgh petunias!"

"You went to Pittsburgh for petunias?" he asked.

"No, look! They're black and gold – Pittsburgh colors!"

"You're hopeless," he said, shaking his head. What did he know? He's a Buffalo fan.

Summer came on, and the petunias spilled proudly out of every container. Even my garden gnomes stood a little taller beside them. When friends came to visit, I proudly showed them my petunias. "They're black and gold, you know." They smiled indulgently and glanced sadly toward Ron.

I found a second shop carrying my petunias at an end-of-season sale. The gentleman I was chatting with in the store mentioned that his wife sent him for a few flowers to fill an empty pot. "How about these?" I asked. "They're black and gold. You know, like the Steelers." The man looked at me with a mix of fear and pity as he backed away. I glanced down and realized I was wearing a Steelers T-shirt. Oh, well, he was probably a New York Jets fan.

Another winter and hockey season came and went. Spring was back in bloom and the Penguins were back in the playoffs. Off I went to the garden store for my petunias. I searched the display of annuals. No black and gold. Were they with the new arrivals? No. Hanging baskets, perhaps? Nope. I picked out some red-and-white petunias, a few snapdragons, and some million bells. At the checkout, I casually asked about the yellow-and-black Phantoms from last year. "Oh, yes, I remember those," the cashier said. "Last year we had a woman who bought them because they were Steeler colors. She was so funny!"

"That was me," I whispered.

"See? I still remember! I thought that was so funny."

She couldn't tell me why they didn't carry them this year. I tried the other garden store, but no luck. I tried the big box store and the local Mennonite farm market. No one had my Pittsburgh petunias. "Maybe all the other fans bought them up," Ron said helpfully. Hmmm – a conspiracy by Montreal Canadiens fans? Could be. I potted up the other flowers. They were pretty enough, I guess, but even my tiny gnomes knew something was missing.

At the end of May, I had an appointment in Rochester. On the way home, I stopped at a garden center. Wandering through the annuals, I saw them – my Pittsburgh petunias! There were four left. I grabbed them all. At the checkout stand, I couldn't stop grinning. "These are black and gold," I told the young cashier. "Pittsburgh colors, like the Steelers and the Penguins."

She gave me a quizzical look and laughed. "That's the most creative excuse I've ever heard for buying flowers! Pittsburgh colors! That's a good one!"

Well, the Penguins didn't win the Stanley Cup this year – but they'll be back. The Pittsburgh Pirates are playing pretty good baseball, and I have high hopes for the Steelers. Maybe I'll find a place that sells chip-chop ham and Iron City beer. Or maybe not. All is good. My containers are filled with black and gold, and my gnomes – and I – are once again standing proud.

SHRUBS, TREES & FOLIAGE PLANTS

- ❀ **Perennial shrub for zones 5-8**
- ❀ **Full sun to part sun**
- ❀ **Happiest in morning sun and afternoon shade**

 Tip Azaleas are best pruned right after they are done blooming. They will put on buds just a few weeks after blooming. If pruning is delayed, next year's flowers will be removed when the plant is trimmed.

There are plenty of yellow azaleas, but this one captures the perfect color for a Steel City Garden. This type of hybrid (Exbury) was created by Baron von Rothschild, who combined other hybrids with stock from around the world at his England estate.

'Klondyke' grows moderately fast, eventually reaching nearly eight feet tall and six feet wide. This is a plant that needs water, especially for the first couple of years until established. Water once a week when rain is scarce. The best way to water any plant is to soak at the base in the morning. This prepares it for the day and allows the leaves to dry off during the day. A few inches of mulch of organic matter like compost, shredded bark or dehydrated manure will keep the soil evenly moist.

I love evergreen azaleas like 'Klondyke.' The winter interest is wonderful, and in the spring when the plant blooms it's a magnet for butterflies and hummingbirds.

WHERE IT WORKS BEST

Azaleas love acidic soil, and in the wild are a woodland understory plant. I never like to see them as foundation plants; so much better on the edge of the forest. They can also act as a great border to block out the neighbor's doublewide. But they're not happy growing in the South. 'Klondyke' is better in a cooler climate.

PESTS AND DISEASES

Aphids, whitefly, scale and fungal diseases can bother azaleas.

Aphids and whitefly: Control with insecticidal soap or horticultural oil.

Scale: try horticultural oil or a dab of rubbing alcohol.

Fungal issues: Use organic fungicides BEFORE signs of damage for best results.

PLANT PARTNERS

Two shrubs that can give a strong, dark backdrop for 'Klondyke's' bright yellow: **'Black Negligee' black bugbane**, and 'Black Lace' elderberry.

BUTTERCUP BUSH
Potentilla

- ❀ Perennial shrub for zones 2-7
- ❀ Full sun to part sun

 Tip The shrub comes in many different colors, including white and red. Put those next to a blueberry and you'll start an All American Garden.

I'll never forget the first time I saw a buttercup bush. It was planted in my best friend's landscape, and the shrub was completely covered with 3/4-inch, bright yellow flowers. The bush started blooming in late summer and kept flowering until fall. That shrub filled with yellow blossoms was quite a sight and whenever I see one in a nursery, I think about that summer day.

Though this plant may be pretty (and certainly attracts the attention of butterflies), it is not fragile. Potentilla are tough, long-lived shrubs when planted where they are happy. And they are deer and drought resistant.

For best results, prune out the oldest stems in late winter when the plant is dormant. This will keep the shrub from getting leggy. Feed in early spring with an organic granular fertilizer.

WHERE IT WORKS BEST

Potentilla loves full sun and well-drained soil. The shrub doesn't need a lot of water, loves the heat and will benefit from some mulch to preserve spring moisture. Put three together in the middle of a border and they will be the stars of the summer garden.

PESTS AND DISEASES

Spider mites can infest the shrubs when the weather gets hot, and some fungal issues can also trouble the plant.

Spider mites: Control with insecticidal soap or horticultural oil.

Fungal issues and powdery mildew: Control with an organic fungicide. Powdery mildew can also be treated with the Cornell mixture (see p. 25).

PLANT PARTNERS

Plant **black sweet potato vines** at the base of the plant and let them intertwine with the shrub. It's a design trick gardeners use with perennial vines, too.

GOLDEN RAIN TREE
Koelreuteria paniculata

 Deciduous tree for zones 5-9

 Full sun

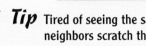 *Tip* Tired of seeing the same old trees in the landscape? Here's one that will make the neighbors scratch their heads and ask where they can get one.

The golden rain tree is underused in North American landscapes. You'll see one here and there, but I think it deserves a place in any garden for both its beauty and toughness.

It's a stunning tree with bright yellow flowers that hang down on clusters that can reach 15 inches long, putting on a wonderful show during the summer. But this is no one trick pony. The flowers give way to cool looking papery seedpods that look like Chinese lanterns. It also has nice fall color, as the foliage turns yellow at the end of the season. This is a fairly small tree, eventually reaching 30 feet tall and wide. It can get a little bigger in warmer climates.

I shot these photographs in England. The one was taken at Windsor Castle and the other shows trees growing across an arbor at Hampton Court. Most of the gardeners who visited England with me thought the golden rain tree arbor was wisteria.

WHERE IT WORKS BEST

The golden rain tree enjoys full sun and will thrive in a variety of soils. It's easy to grow and long lived where it's happy. This Asian native has been known to escape cultivation and in some areas is considered invasive. I have a gardening friend who can't stand the tree because it sends up suckers everywhere. She fears she'll never get rid of it. Beauty is truly in the eye of the beholder.

PESTS AND DISEASES

No serious pests or diseases.

PLANT PARTNERS

Cornflower, 'Black Lace' elderberry and black elephant ear

- ❀ Tropical plant hardy in zones 9-10
- ❀ Full sun to part sun

 Tip Some gardeners put their hibiscus into dormancy over the winter, instead of growing it as a houseplant. Put the plant in a cool, dark space and let it dry out, watering about once a month to keep it alive.

I have a friend who grew 200 tropical hibiscus on his patio, planning to present his landscape on a local gardening tour. The night before, a herd of deer took each plant down to three inches. After wiping his tears, he kept growing hibiscus, but always sprayed them with a deer repellent. If deer are a problem, keep the plants protected while they are outside during the summer.

Tropical hibiscus have big, beautiful flowers in a rainbow of colors and shapes. We're most interested in the yellow blooms, and there are lots of them.

The plants can't take any cold weather; they go out in the garden once all danger of frost has passed. They go back inside before the first frost of the season. Sometimes they grow into large trees and become difficult to move in and out. I buy them small, and then I can grow them for years until the fateful fall day when they get too big.

WHERE IT WORKS BEST

Tropical hibiscus work best in containers so they can be transported in and out according to the weather. Give them a spot in full sun. Feed the plant an organic, liquid fertilizer every couple of weeks.

PESTS AND DISEASES

Aphids, spider mites, whiteflies and scale are the three worst pests for tropical hibiscus. Fungal issues can also affect hibiscus.

Aphids, spider mites and whiteflies: Insecticidal soap or horticultural oil are both great organic controls for the pests. Be sure to coat the insects with the soap or oil; don't forget the undersides of the leaves.

Fungal issues: Use an organic fungicide.

PLANT PARTNERS

None needed.

Magnolia 'Sunburst'

- Ornamental tree for zones 4-8
- Part sun, part shade

Tip These are great trees for urban gardens, as they are tolerant of pollution.

'Sunburst' is a wonderful magnolia with five-inch-long, canary yellow flowers. When the tree flowers in early spring it looks like lemon colored candles glowing in the landscape. The foliage is beautiful too, which begins as a bronze, purple color then fades to green for the rest of the season.

When full grown, 'Sunburst' will be nearly 30 feet tall and 20 feet or more in diameter. The tree is deciduous and will lose its leaves at the end of the season. Magnolias can be problematic in colder climates. The buds often swell early in the season and then are killed by a late frost. To avoid this I try to site them in a protected spot on the east or north side of the house.

WHERE IT WORKS BEST

Try and find a site that allows the tree to be protected from wind. A magnolia doesn't like competition either, so give it a space of its own. They love morning sun and afternoon shade.

A good, well-drained, acidic soil filled with organic matter will make the 'Sunburst' magnolia happy.

PESTS AND DISEASES

Magnolia scale and fungal issues can affect this tree.

Magnolia scale: This is probably the worst pest to attack the tree. Use horticultural oil or rubbing alcohol to combat the pest.

Fungal issues: Treat magnolias that are affected by using an organic fungicide.

PLANT PARTNERS

Black perennial plants, like **'Black Negligee' black bugbane** and 'Black Lace' elderberry

Rosa 'Noalesca' ('Flower Carpet Yellow')

- Perennial shrub for zones 5-10
- Full sun

 Tip The organic, granular fertilizer Rosetone should be applied once a month to roses. It will keep roses growing strong and healthy.

There are a multitude of different yellow roses, but none tougher than the 'Flower Carpet Yellow.' The plant is filled with buttercup-yellow flowers from spring through the end of fall. The flowers are a pretty semi-double and are arranged in clusters of five or six held over shiny green leaves.

One of the great things about newer roses like 'Flower Carpet Yellow' is that it's disease resistant. It's simple to grow and shouldn't need fungicides to keep it healthy. Another great thing about this particular plant is that it is bred to drop old flowers, so it does not need deadheading. In the dormant period, late winter into early spring, about a third of the plant should be cut back.

If you're worried about growing roses because you've heard they're fussy, try 'Flower Carpet Yellow.' It's a winner.

WHERE IT WORKS BEST

Full sun and well drained soil is what roses need. Make sure the planting hole is filled with organic matter like compost. Roses like to be mulched to keep the soil evenly moist.

PESTS AND DISEASES

You may not find many problems with 'Flower Carpet Yellow,' but here's what you can do if problems arise.

Aphids: Control with insecticidal soap or horticultural oil.

Sawfly larvae: They can be easily controlled with Captain Jack's Deadbug Brew.

Black spot and other fungal issues: Prevented with an organic fungicide. Use the Cornell mixture (see p. 25) for black spot.

PLANT PARTNERS

Black and yellow petunias, black bugbane and black elderberry

GOLDEN VARIEGATED SAGE

Salvia officinalis 'Icterina'

- ❀ Perennial herb for zones 6-9
- ❀ Full sun to part sun

 Tip Combine golden variegated sage with other flowering plants in a border, bed or container as a wonderful surprise for garden visitors.

Golden variegated sage shouldn't just be relegated to the herb garden. This beautiful plant has golden foliage and will bloom with pretty blue flowers that are worthy of a place in any garden.

Even though it's often grown as an ornamental, sage is a well-loved edible plant. Rub a leaf between your fingers to release the unmistakable aroma reminiscent of Thanksgiving dinner. The herb is best used fresh, but can also be dried. The plant can grow to two feet tall and a foot or so wide.

This is a great choice for a container, too. To create a pretty scene in your garden, use it as a filler around something spectacular. Hummingbirds, butterflies and bees will be attracted to the flowers, completing the peaceful picture of your black and gold garden.

WHERE IT WORKS BEST

Golden variegated sage is one tough plant. It's heat and drought tolerant, loves full sun and will thrive in average garden soil. When it grows in soil amended with compost, however, it will give you more sage than you could ever use.

PESTS AND DISEASES

This plant is mostly free of pests and diseases.

PLANT PARTNERS

Black mondo grass and black and gold petunias

BLACK BUGBANE (Black Cohosh)

Actaea simplex (formerly *Cimicifuga simplex*) 'Black Negligee'

- ❁ Perennial plant for zones 3-9
- ❁ Full sun to part shade

 Tip Bugbane can be divided every five years to produce more plants.

There are many black bugbane varieties that will fit the bill for the Steel City Garden if 'Black Negligee' can't be found, but it's the blackest yet of the cultivars.

This is a late bloomer (just like me) that loves good soil and plenty of water. When some of the other plants in the garden have reached their peak, black bugbane is just getting started. In August or September, fragrant white flowers tinged with purple reach up to five feet, attracting butterflies to the garden. Each plant can spread up to three feet around. What's nice is that even though the flowers are so tall, they don't need staking.

While bugbane is appreciated for its tall, bottle brush-like flowers, for most of the season gardeners can enjoy the deeply cut purple/black foliage, combined with its dark stems.

WHERE IT WORKS BEST

This unusual but beautiful perennial plant will naturalize easily when given the right conditions. I have some growing in a woodland garden and it's slowly working its way through the bed, to my delight. It's wonderful used in the back of a woodland border in large groups. Seven to eleven of these plants growing in concert are a showstopper.

PESTS AND DISEASES

The plant has no serious threat from pests or diseases, except maybe the occasional snail or slug.

The name bugbane refers to an old belief that the odor of its flowers can repel certain insects (its former Latin name, *Cimicifuga,* means bug repellent).

PLANT PARTNERS

Yellow shade-loving annuals like **pansies**; try corydalis and bidens too.

Ophiopogon planiscapus 'Ebony Knight'

- 🌼 Perennial plant for zones 5-10
- 🌼 Full sun to part sun

 Tip Divide the plant every couple of seasons to keep it growing strong. Older spring foliage can be removed in favor of new leaves.

'Ebony Knight' is a great plant for the black and gold garden. The grass-like foliage is a deep purplish black and is the perfect foil for anything yellow.

It's a slow grower that makes a great ground cover, edge or border. It actually puts on black berries, which are hidden in the evergreen leaves. The birds love the berries and will seek the plant out for one of their favorite snacks. The berries appear right after the bell-shaped, lavender flowers. The plant is also a great weed suppressor, as it forms a thick, impenetrable mat.

Despite its name, black mondo grass is not really a grass and has fat, quarter-inch leaves. When it's happy, the foliage reaches nearly 10 inches, but when the plant is stressed, the leaves only reach three to four inches. There are many different types of black mondo grass.

WHERE IT WORKS BEST

'Ebony Knight' and other mondo grasses aren't fussy, but do need watering during the first year to get established. Once it is, however, black mondo grass is a long-lived perennial. It will do fine as an understory plant in the shade and can take the sun, too. If you do plant it in the sun where rain isn't abundant, it will need to be watered once a week. This plant is especially happy in acidic soil with plenty of organic matter.

PESTS AND DISEASES

'Ebony Knight' and other black mondo grasses are largely free of pests, but they do suffer from root rot, probably the most serious disease your plants can face. To avoid it, be sure the plants have plenty of drainage.

PLANT PARTNERS

Marigolds, bidens and lantana

Sambucus nigra 'Black Lace'

🌼 Perennial
shrub for
zones 4-7

🌼 Full sun to
part sun

 Tip Plant several 'Black Lace' elderberries in a row to make a dramatic privacy hedge.

Who would have thought plant breeders could turn the common elderberry bush into a spectacular landscape specimen? They've certainly done that with 'Black Lace' and other cultivars.

The dark purple foliage on this plant is finely cut, making it look like a Japanese maple. For our purposes, we're growing 'Black Lace' for its foliage, but the creamy pink flowers are pretty and attract butterflies. After flowering, the plant puts on blackish red berries, which the birds love. See page 117 for tasty things you can do with the berries.

Reaching eight feet high (spreading as wide as it is tall), it takes well to pruning and is deer resistant. 'Black Lace' is tough. It loves moist soil but will tolerate some dryness. It needs full sun to have the best color. Prune hard during the first few years, right after blooming, as it flowers on old wood. Use a good organic liquid fertilizer once a month.

WHERE IT WORKS BEST

Usually grown as a landscape specimen, 'Black Lace' can also be a very dramatic container plant. Choose a beautiful large container and use the plant as the thriller in the middle of the pot. Add some yellow annuals to spill over the edges for the perfect black and gold container garden.

PESTS AND DISEASES

Elderberry is bothered by spider mites, powdery mildew and other fungal diseases.

Aphids and spider mites: Control with insecticidal soap or horticultural oil. Two or three applications should do the trick.

Powdery mildew and other fungal issues: Use organic fungicides. The Cornell mixture (see p. 25) is my favorite control for powdery mildew.

PLANT PARTNERS

Lantana and bidens

ELEPHANT EAR
Colocasia esculenta 'Black Royal Hawaiian Eye'

- ❁ Grown as an annual, houseplant or perennial in zones 7-9

- ❁ Full sun to part shade, will survive in full shade

 Tip Grow 'Black Royal Hawaiian Eye' or other cultivars in a container and bring it into the house during cold weather, giving it a little window light.

Elephant ear is a great tropical plant with huge black leaves tinged in purple. This fast-growing statement plant is grown for its expansive foliage, which can reach four feet in height. It thrives in moist soil and full to partial shade.

Be careful where you plant elephant ear, however, because all parts of the plant are poisonous if ingested. It is not advisable to have in a garden with children or pets.

Elephant ear can be sold as either a tuber or a potted plant, and there are many different varieties of elephant ear that are dark purple or black. 'Black Royal Hawaiian Eye' is especially conducive to a Steel City Garden, but any dark variety of this plant is suitable.

An interesting fact about this unusual plant is that the Hawaiian food poi is made from the tubers of colocasias. The tubers, when steamed and properly processed to make poi, are safe and nutritious to eat.

WHERE IT WORKS BEST

Planted in groups of three or five, 'Black Royal Hawaiian Eye' makes a bold statement in any garden. This plant prefers a cool, moist spot. Boggy areas and water gardens are the perfect location.

PESTS AND DISEASES

Aphids, whiteflies and spider mites: Control with insecticidal soap or horticultural oil.

Soft rot, bacterial blight, corm and root rots: Organic fungicides can help with these common blights, but it's important to purchase disease-free plants and tubers.

PLANT PARTNERS

Bidens and corydalis

SWEET POTATO VINE

Ipomoea batatas, **many cultivars**

- ❀ Annual bedding plant
- ❀ Full sun to part sun

 Tip The tuber is technically edible, but bred as a bedding plant. I've never tasted one; I've been told they aren't too tasty. It can be saved over the winter in the same way dahlias and caladiums are stored.

We are used to seeing the chartreuse varieties of the sweet potato vine spilling out of containers. The black varieties aren't used as much, but make a great foil for anything yellow.

They are usually bought already started in plastic pots at the nursery. Sweet potato vines love warm weather and look good in containers and hanging baskets as they trail down from the pot. The plants can also be let to sprawl as a groundcover.

There are some with smaller heart-shaped leaves, and others with larger, lobed foliage. Ipomoea batatas 'Blackie' has the larger-lobed leaves and is a good choice for any gardener. Ipomoea batatas 'Black Heart' has smaller heart-shaped leaves on vines that can get nearly five feet long.

WHERE IT WORKS BEST

Sweet potato vines will grow just about anywhere. They love full sun and lots of heat but will happily trail out of containers in the shade. They are easy to grow and look nice combined with yellow flowers or vines.

PESTS AND DISEASES

Aphids, a variety of beetles and caterpillars will affect the vine, and sometimes fungal disease can be a problem.

Aphids: Insecticidal soap or horticultural oil are both great organic controls for the pests. Be sure to coat the insects and both sides of the leaves.

Beetles and caterpillars: Captain Jack's Deadbug Brew will work on chewing pests. It's organic and safe for the good bugs (which don't chew).

PLANT PARTNERS

Yellow annuals such as **bidens** and chartreuse sweet potato vines

BERNIE PINTAR'S GARDEN

Bernie Pintar's East Pittsburgh garden is a work of art…literally. He's a wonderful artist who works with clay and other mediums. Bernie took one city lot a friend lent him and created a magical space where he gardens with three friends.

Walking through the gate, summer visitors are greeted by trees laden with pretty pink peaches, nearly ripe. These trees are loaded; in fact, during a summer's storm one cracked in half under the weight of the fruit.

He's growing lots of black and gold plants, too. Sunflowers, black beans, yellow beans, black fennel, 'Black Krim' tomatoes, eggplant, black sweet potato vine and more.

Bernie and I sit out of the sun in a quaint little area he built, and take in the garden together. All the way across the lot and up high along the road stands a 10-foot-tall sunflower. "Look at that beauty up there just looking at us. That's got both black and gold, brother," he says with a laugh.

Everything from the Swiss chard to the tomatoes is thriving, and that puts a big smile on this 62-year-old gardener's face. The compost pile is huge and it's obvious from the size of his plants what he's using to keep them so healthy.

He didn't start gardening until 2007. When asked why, he pauses, looks quizzically and says, "Because that's what Hunkys do. You're looking at an old fashioned Hunky garden," referring to his Eastern European heritage. "My father was Slovak and my mother was from Croatia; that's as Hunky as it gets," he laughs. "You know what I call this garden? Heaven on earth, an artist's garden."

He's created art and put it all over the garden. There's a sculpture made of thick, rusted railroad spikes and a circular column of bricks he calls "The Belly of Mother Earth." Along the top of the bricks are pieces of black coal. What do they represent? "Whatever you want them to," he says. When I remark that it's a celebration of old Pittsburgh, he smiles. "Brother, I like the way you're talking."

But when the artist is asked what's the best thing for him about being in this garden, without missing a beat he says, "It creates peace."

And what gardener wouldn't want that.

FRUITS & VEGGIES

LEMONS
Citrus limon, Citrus x meyeri

- ✿ **Tropical fruit**
- ✿ **Full sun to part sun**

Tip A ripe lemon will almost fall off the tree when picked. If it resists, it's not ready yet.

Unless you live in the warmest areas of the country, lemons are grown indoors in the winter and put outside all summer. If that seems like a hassle, you can always just buy the fruit at the grocery store, but lemon lovers can get fresh fruit with a little bit of work and knowledge.

One of the most wonderful things about growing citrus indoors is the intoxicating fragrance of the flowers. The Meyer lemon, a lemon hybrid, is sweeter than typical lemons, and are especially popular for inside cultivation. (The Meyers shown on the facing page are growing in a Southern California garden.)

To keep your plant comfortable, choose a container that is at least 15 gallons, bigger if you can move it. Use a good planting mix when the tree is indoors and fertilize often, once it is outdoors for the summer. Keep in mind that if the lemon plant blooms inside, it will need to be hand pollinated in order to produce fruit.

WHERE IT WORKS BEST

Place your tree in front of a big, south-facing window to keep it happy in the winter. For outside growing, find a site with full sun.

PESTS AND DISEASES

Lemon trees can suffer from aphids, mealybugs, spider mites and, later, thrips and scale. Lemons are pretty free of disease when grown indoors, but they can get some fungal issues.

PLANT PARTNERS

None needed.

Rubus, many species and cultivars

✿ **Perennial plant**

✿ **Full sun to part sun**

 Tip Blackberries have many health benefits, including antioxidants, and are thought to reduce cardiovascular disease and lower cholesterol.

Growing up in the 1960s in the country was a wonderful experience. As kids, we ran wild all summer long. In July, we'd spend day after day picking wild blackberries. When our buckets were full, we took them down to Mrs. Russell's house where she turned them into sweet tasting, wonderful pies. Those wild berries were tiny in comparison to the cultivated varieties available now. Some new varieties offer thornless canes, though those sweet pies were worth all the scratches we endured in our picking adventures.

Any one of today's many species and cultivars would be perfect to add a black accent to your Steel City Garden. Thornless 'Triple Crown' produces lots of big blackberries. 'Chester Thornless,' from Peaceful Valley Farm and Garden Supply, is easy to pick, very hardy, prolific, and produces berries towards the end of the season. 'Kiowa' has plenty of thorns, but it boasts giant berries that ripen early in the summer.

WHERE IT WORKS BEST

Blackberries long for full sun but will produce with a little bit of shade. Hardy varieties can be planted in the fall or early spring. All varieties will benefit from fertile soil amended with compost.

Many gardeners support their vines with a homemade trellis. If that works for you, you'll find a good selection of designs online.

PESTS AND DISEASES

Borers will occasionally attack the canes, and the blackberries are susceptible to various fungal diseases.

Borers: Remove canes with borer damage. They won't often do enough damage to a patch to cause serious problems.

Fungal issues: Be sure the plants are in well-drained, loamy soil. Serenade works for many fungal problems.

PLANT PARTNERS

None needed.

ELDERBERRIES

Sambucus, **many species and cultivars**

- ❀ **Perennial plant**
- ❀ **Full sun to part sun**

 Tip Elderberries contain more phosphorus and potassium than any other temperate fruit crop. The fruit is also rich in vitamin C.

Elderberries are probably more popular today as ornamental plants than as fruit producers. However, many plants grown for the landscape also produce tasty berries, and elderberries, with their tart fruit, are no exception. (See page 102 for a stunning black-foliaged elderberry shrub.) Here's another reason to enjoy this plant: Its flowers are wonderfully fragrant.

Let's talk about growing elderberries as an edible crop. What do you think of when the word 'elderberry' comes up? I think of wine – and I've had some wonderful homemade elderberry wine – but the fruit is also good for pies, jellies and jams.

The berries need to be processed before eating. They are tart, to say the least, and are often regarded as inedible without some sugar.

WHERE IT WORKS BEST

Elderberries are easy to grow. Full sun is best, but they're not fussy. Plant them in the spring and make sure they get plenty of water. This is especially important in the first year, as they are shallow rooted. Well-drained soil and a layer of mulch will keep the soil evenly moist.

Spread an application of compost around the drip line to keep elderberries happy and producing at their best.

PESTS AND DISEASES

Borers will sometimes attack the canes, and elderberries are also susceptible to powdery mildew.

Borers: Remove canes with borer damage. These pests won't often do enough damage to a patch to cause serious problems.

Powdery Mildew: Serenade or the Cornell mixture (see p. 25) will work well in controlling this fungal disease.

PLANT PARTNERS

None needed.

GRAPES

Vitis vinifera and other cultivars

- ❀ Perennial vine
- ❀ Full sun to part sun

 Tip Winemaking kits are a great resource to help avoid common mistakes with homemade wine. If you've ever been served homemade wine that might be better as paint thinner, you know what I mean.

Have you ever tried grape pie? It may sound weird but, trust me, it's awesome. Of course, grapes are useful for other things besides pie, which makes this versatile plant perfect for the garden. If you're interested in growing this versatile plant, 'Concord' is still one of the most popular varieties for home cultivation.

Once established and pruned correctly, grape vines will outlive the gardener. I had the pleasure of seeing one of the world's oldest vines at Hampton Court Palace in London, England. It's the largest vine in the world, dates back to 1769 and, yes, still produces grapes.

To learn how to care for this tough and vigorous plant, visit someone who has been successful and learn how he makes his plants thrive. This is especially important for learning how to prune, which is difficult to explain but easy to demonstrate. Once you watch someone prune grapes, you'll know exactly what to do.

WHERE IT WORKS BEST

You will need decent soil, support for the vines, education in pruning and an organic fungal spraying regime. Oh yeah, and full sun, too. It may sound complicated, but I've also known gardeners without any of the above who harvested grapes every year. Don't be afraid of making a mistake. Grapes are hardy, so any problems can likely be fixed next season.

PESTS AND DISEASES

Fungal diseases are the main problem for grapes, but they are also plagued by the pests below:

Mealybugs, thrips, spider mites: Use organic insecticidal soap or horticultural oil.

Scale: Use horticultural oil or rubbing alcohol.

Japanese beetles: Use Captain Jack's Deadbug Brew.

Fungal issues: Spray grapes religiously during the season with an organic fungicide.

PLANT PARTNERS

None. Grapes should be grown on their own.

GARDEN HUCKLEBERRY

Solanum scabrum, S. burbankii and *S. melanocerasum*

- Annual vegetable
- Full sun to part sun

Tip Before harvesting, wait until the gloss on the berry fades and it gets a little soft.

Here's an underused and fun plant for the vegetable garden that has caused a bit of controversy over the years. Is the garden huckleberry a fruit or a vegetable? It's sometimes referred to as the wonderberry, which implies that it is a fruit, but it is also not related to true huckleberries, which grow as a woody shrub. So which is it? Since it's the cousin of tomatoes, and tomatoes are officially a fruit, I'm saying garden huckleberry is a fruit.

The garden huckleberry makes blueberry-size black berries that are bitter at first and sweeten a little as they ripen. They are most often used in making jams, jellies, pies and preserves. One plant often produces enough berries to make one pie. I know some gardeners who eat them right off the plant when they are very ripe and thus at their sweetest. How much sugar to add for cooking is up to your personal taste; check out some recipes online for added guidance and some fresh ideas.

WHERE IT WORKS BEST

Huckleberries are grown just like tomatoes and need their culture. It's ok to allow them to sprawl in the garden, or you can grow them along a fence. Give them fertile soil and plenty of water, and they will produce thousands of pretty black berries. Seeds can be found from Baker Creek Heirloom Seeds and other sources.

PESTS AND DISEASES

Largely pest and disease free, although slugs will eat the foliage.

Slugs: Control with organic bait like Sluggo, trap with stale beer, or hand pick.

PLANT PARTNERS

Lantana and bidens

🌼 **Annual vegetable**

🌼 **Full sun to part sun**

 Tip If you've never tried pole beans, give it a shot. They need some support to grow on and take a little longer to get going, but they have a longer harvest time and are much easier to pick.

Beans are an important part of any vegetable garden, but yellow beans grown alongside deep purple beans can make a Steel City Garden statement. There's nothing easier to grow, as long as you can keep the rabbits and groundhogs at bay.

Pole beans like 'Gold Marie Vining,' 'French Gold' and 'Kentucky Wonder Wax' are my favorites. I'm also growing a rainbow mix with 'Blue Lake,' 'Yellow Pole Wax' and 'Purple Peacock' from Renee's Garden, that gets me close to black and gold.

There are also plenty of bush beans in yellow colors, like 'Golden Wax' and 'Gold Mine.' Dark purple bush beans, like 'Purple Queen' and 'Royalty Purple Bush,' are as close to black as you can get.

WHERE IT WORKS BEST

Beans love full sun but will produce with half a day of sunshine. Plant them in good compost and you'll be picking more beans than even your friends can eat. Beans are almost always direct sowed in the garden.

PESTS AND DISEASES

Lots of pests and funguses love beans.

Aphids and thrips: Use insecticidal soap or horticultural oil.

Rabbits, groundhogs: For both, use fencing or repellent. For persistent groundhogs, trap or kill. Sorry.

Mexican bean beetles: Crush eggs, handpick larvae, and use Captain Jack's Deadbug Brew on adults.

Fungal issues: Use Serenade.

PLANT PARTNERS

None needed.

- ✿ Biennial vegetable
- ✿ Full sun to part sun

 Tip Don't forget about the tasty, healthy greens! 'Golden Beet' is especially flavorful in salads and won't bleed like red beets.

There are lots of yellow or golden cultivars of beets, but this heirloom from the early 1800s is my favorite. I never liked beets until I started growing them for my wife. She finally cajoled me into trying some roasted 'Detroit Dark Red' beets and I became the biggest beet supporter on the planet.

Check out the YouTube video, "Give Beets A Chance," that I did with my friend and radio partner Jessica Walliser. We started a campaign to get beets into the White House garden, and it worked!

Beets want full sun, but will produce with around six hours of daylight. Plant them early in the spring as soon as the soil is workable. Beets can overwinter with protection in cold climates. In winter, I love to harvest them under a thick layer of straw. Be sure to amend the planting area with lots of compost. Beets can be picky about soil pH, so have your soil tested to get the pH right.

WHERE IT WORKS BEST

Although beets are direct sowed into the garden, they work well when started in six packs. Beet seed is actually many seeds inside the seedpod, so it's important to thin them when they sprout to give them enough space. Beets need space to make their tasty root. Seeding them in flats makes the thinning much easier. I put a couple of crops in during the season. The last one is sowed around the first of August in my zone 6 garden.

PESTS AND DISEASES

Beets are pretty pest and disease free. Sometimes, aphids, flea beetles or slugs will get after the foliage.

Aphids: Control with insecticidal soap or horticultural oil.

Flea beetles: Not a huge concern of mine, but Captain Jack's Deadbug Brew should do the trick.

Slugs: Control with an organic slug bait like Sluggo, trap with stale beer, or hand pick.

PLANT PARTNERS

'Round Black Spanish' radish

- Biennial vegetable
- Full sun to part sun

 Tip Sow another crop of carrots in mid-summer for a fall harvest. Carrots will winter over in the garden under a thick layer of straw and be fresh during a winter thaw. Carrot seedlings removed for thinning make great additions to any salad.

Carrots and radishes go together in a vegetable garden, and I have the perfect black and gold pairing for you: these 'Amarillo Yellow' carrots, coupled with 'Round Black Spanish' radishes (on page 132). Both are reliable heirlooms from Baker Creek Heirloom Seeds.

Prepare a bed – about five feet by four feet – by adding a quarter yard or more of compost on top and smoothing it out with a hoe. Spread the carrot seed across the compost, rake it in, water and wait. (The same growing instructions apply if you're planting the black radish seeds along with the carrot seeds. The radishes will sprout first and should be thinned to make room for the carrots.) Either way, you'll end up with a carpet of vegetables. Using pure compost will give them all the nutrients they need despite the confined space. 'Amarillo Yellow' carrot will be ready for harvest in about 75 days. The roots will reach eight inches long and are crunchy and juicy.

WHERE IT WORKS BEST

Carrots need full sun, but will make roots with only six hours of daylight. They enjoy soft, fertile soil and deep compost to allow the roots to grow straight and deep.

For fresh spring carrots, prepare the bed in the fall and sow at the end of winter. The first year I did this, the carrots sprouted in early April (my radishes three weeks earlier).

PESTS AND DISEASES

Carrot fly is probably the worst pest for this crop.

Carrot fly: Cover the newly sprouted carrots with a floating row cover. This spun-bound, translucent fabric separates the carrots from the fly.

PLANT PARTNERS

'Round Black Spanish' radish

- Annual vegetable
- Full sun to part sun

 Tip If you don't have room for your squash to spread out, you can grow the vines up a trellis. That keeps the fruit off the ground and away from cucumber beetles.

What vegetable garden would be complete without summer squash? As far as shapes, sizes and colors are concerned, summer squash covers a lot of ground. For the Steel City Garden, we're looking at yellow cultivars.

Insect resistant and prolific, 'Lemon Squash' is an heirloom variety that produces yellow fruit resembling lemons. The 'Early Prolific Straightneck' Squash was the 1938 All-America Selection, and it's just as good today. Great for grilling and tastes wonderful. The small "patty pan" varieties are delicious too.

WHERE IT WORKS BEST

Like most vegetables, summer squash loves a lot of sun but will produce with half a day of sunshine. These heavy feeders will benefit from growing in good soil, and they love compost.

I direct sow the seeds in the ground after the last frost, but some gardeners start with plants. Summer squash resents root disturbance, so plants will be happier when transplanted in peat pots, which will rot away during the season.

PESTS AND DISEASES

There are plenty of squash pests and fungal diseases.

Cucumber beetles: Use Captain Jack's Deadbug Brew.

Squash bugs: Squash the eggs, handpick the bugs, cover plants with a floating row cover until they bloom.

Powdery mildew: Use the Cornell mixture (see p. 25) or another organic fungicide.

PLANT PARTNERS

Purple bush beans

- Biennial vegetable
- Full sun to part sun

 Tip Pick the leaves when they are small for the sweetest taste and most tender texture. Remove the center stalk on bigger leaves and cook them separately, the same way you'd cook asparagus.

I don't think I've ever had a garden without Swiss chard. For those of us who can't grow spinach because it bolts as soon as the weather gets hot, chard is a great substitute, since it will produce all season long. In my zone-6 garden, Swiss chard will grow well into winter and may even survive until spring, with a little protection.

Swiss chard is actually from the beet family, cultivated purely for its beautiful and tasty foliage. The yellow varieties (the stems carry the yellow color) are often sold in rainbow mixes like 'Bright Lights.' If you're just looking for yellow, you can find seeds for 'Bright Yellow' or 'Canary Yellow,'" sold separately.

WHERE IT WORKS BEST

Swiss chard loves full sun but will produce in part sun, too. Beds improved with compost will have your Swiss chard producing huge, three-foot-tall leaves through fall and maybe well into winter.

I love to sow seeds at the end of winter and again in mid-summer when space opens up after I've harvested garlic and other spring greens.

PESTS AND DISEASES

Swiss chard is sometimes bothered by slugs and Cercospora leaf spot, a fungal disease that forms light brown patches on the leaves, caused by rainy, humid seasons.

Slugs: Control with organic baits like Sluggo, trap with stale beer, or handpick.

Cercospora: Good spacing will help, and after removing infected leaves the plant will send up replacements from the center.

PLANT PARTNERS

Black tomatoes and 'Round Black Spanish' radish

RADISHES
Raphanus sativus 'Round Black Spanish'

- ✿ Annual vegetable
- ✿ Full sun to part sun

 Tip Sow another crop in mid-summer for a fall harvest. Radishes grow best in cool conditions so, if some don't head up, let them go. The seedpods are delicious (especially in salads).

When you think of vegetables, you usually don't picture them as black, but this unusual 'Round Black Spanish' radish seed is a fun black addition to a Steel City vegetable garden. (See the 'Amarillo Yellow' carrot on page 126, for a perfect plant partner. They're great in bed together.)

To prepare the bed – about five feet by four feet – add a quarter yard of compost on top and smooth it out with a hoe. Spread the radish seed across the compost, rake it in, water and wait. This technique will create a carpet of vegetables. Pure compost will give the radishes (and carrots, if grown together) all the nutrients they need despite the confined space.

'Round Black Spanish' can be pulled when small, but can also be left in the soil; they will mature to a full five inches across. The spicy veggie has a black skin and pure white flesh; it will store well in winter.

WHERE IT WORKS BEST

Radishes need full sun, but will make roots with only six hours of daylight. They enjoy soft fertile soil and deep compost to allow the roots to grow straight and deep.

For fresh spring radishes, prepare the bed in the fall and sow at the end of winter. The first year I did this, the radishes sprouted on St. Patrick's Day (my carrots three weeks later).

PESTS AND DISEASES

They'll fight off anything. Just be sure to rotate where they grow each season to avoid some of the soil-borne pests.

Flea beetles: Not a serious concern, but they can get after the foliage. Captain Jack's Dead Bugbrew will help control them. Spreading diatomaceous earth will also work.

PLANT PARTNERS

'Amarillo Yellow' carrot

- Annual vegetable
- Full sun to part sun

Tip Go beyond eggplant Parmesan when using the fruit in the kitchen. Baba ghanoush and ratatouille just scratch the surface of eggplant's culinary possibilities.

Eggplants are among the most beautiful vegetables in the garden, largely due to their variety of colors. We're interested in the darkest purples, which for our purposes look black, but there are also a few bright yellow varieties that would look excellent in a Steel City Garden.

Don't worry that this tasty vegetable will be too difficult to manage. If you can grow tomatoes and peppers, eggplants will be a cinch.

'Ichiban,' one variety of black eggplant, produces a 10-inch-long, thin fruit with wonderful flavor. It is dark purple, prolific and will keep producing fruit well into the fall. 'Ichiban' is only one of countless black varieties that differ greatly in the size and amount of fruit they produce. For a yellow variety, 'Thai Yellow Egg' (or 'Golden Egg') eggplant produces lots of egg-sized bright yellow fruits that light up the vegetable garden.

WHERE IT WORKS BEST

Eggplants like it warm and sunny, just like peppers and tomatoes. They can be planted at the same time tomatoes go in the ground. Eggplants are great in containers and make a nice ornamental plant, too. The big, pretty flowers are impressive, and the colorful fruit works well alongside flowers. Good garden soil amended with compost is a must.

PESTS AND DISEASES

Eggplants are a magnet for flea beetles. They are also susceptible to many fungal issues that plague tomatoes and peppers.

Flea beetles: To keep them off the plant, cover it with a floating row cover, which must be removed when the eggplants begin to flower.

Fungal issues: Mulching, proper spacing and the use of organic fungicides will keep eggplants happy.

PLANT PARTNERS

Yellow and **black tomatoes** and yellow and black peppers

- Annual vegetable
- Full sun to part sun

Tip Many varieties can take a long time to come to fruition. If you have a shorter season, look for bell peppers, which mature quickly.

No vegetable garden is complete without peppers: sweet peppers, stuffing peppers, super hot peppers and everything in between. Most peppers will begin green then change to stunning colors as they ripen.

'Purple Beauty' ripens to a dark purple, almost black, setting fruit prolifically on three-foot-tall, stocky plants. There are also plenty of black hot peppers, like the often ornamental 'Black Pearl.' 'Limon' (or 'Lemon Drop') is a wonderful yellow hot pepper from Peru – a short, bushy plant filled with two-inch-long hot peppers that have a citrusy flavor. This pepper will wake you up!

'Corno di Toro Giallo' is an heirloom Italian yellow sweet pepper. I love to roast these on a charcoal grill and stuff them with exotic cheeses and dried meats (that I'm not supposed to eat). Life is short. Enjoy the garden's bounty.

WHERE IT WORKS BEST

Peppers like it hot and sunny. Don't skimp on the soil or compost; a balanced organic fertilizer will help them grow strong. They like a nice layer of mulch once the soil warms up. Hot peppers can be grown as ornamentals in combination with flowers. Peppers also work well as container plants.

PESTS AND DISEASES

Peppers suffer from some of the same problems as tomatoes, plus a few more.

Blossom end rot: Mulch and keep the soil evenly moist.

Fungal diseases: Use same controls as for tomatoes (see page 139).

Aphids and whiteflies: Use insecticidal soap or horticultural oil.

Chewing pests: Use Captain Jack's Deadbug Brew.

PLANT PARTNERS

None needed.

Solanum lycopersicum

- ❀ Annual vegetable
- ❀ Full sun to part sun

Tip Plants put in the ground early can be more susceptible to fungal diseases than those planted a little later. To avoid problems, give each plant plenty of space for air circulation, at least three feet between plants. Grow tomatoes up on stakes or in cages to keep the plants off the ground. At the time of planting do these things: Mulch (it stops fungal spores from splashing up – though the soil won't warm up as quickly). Remove some of the lower leaves. Fungal spores can't reach a leaf that isn't there...right? Grow resistant varieties.

Everyone knows there is nothing better than a home-grown tomato; it is garden perfection. There's also nothing like standing in the garden barefoot, feasting on warm, tiny 'Black Cherry' tomatoes.

I've fallen in love with black varieties, including 'Japanese Black Trifele,' 'Black Krim,' 'Paul Robeson,' 'Cherokee Purple,' and more. They aren't really black, more like dark purple, but they are wonderful. Each one has its own special flavor and texture. I find they store well at the end of the season, too. As for yellow tomatoes, 'Lemon Boy,' 'Snow White Cherry,' 'Yellow Pear,' 'Dr. Wyche,' 'Yellow Mortgage Lifter' and others are wonderful. ('Snow White Cherry' barely turns yellow, but it's one of my all-time favorites, thus must be included.) I love to feed these to children who've never seen a tomato that wasn't red. It's such a leap of faith for them try these "strange" looking tomatoes. Those brave enough to try are rewarded with a plethora of diverse tomato flavors.

WHERE IT WORKS BEST

Contrary to popular belief, full sun isn't the only place tomatoes will grow. Sure, they will be stocky and happy out in the sun, but the plant will also produce plenty of tomatoes in part sun. The vines will stretch for light and will need some extra support. I use my homemade compost in each planting hole. Give tomatoes great soil and they will provide you with more fruit than a "normal" family can enjoy.

PESTS AND DISEASES

Besides fungal issues, tomatoes can be subject to chewing pests, aphids and whiteflies – though tomatoes usually outgrow the pests.

Fungal issues: Remove affected foliage and control with Serenade. Identify the disease first; late blight is always fatal.

Chewing pests: Use Captain Jack's Deadbug Brew.

Aphids and whiteflies: Control with insecticidal soap or horticultural oil.

PLANT PARTNERS

None needed.

THE JANOSKI GARDEN

JoAnn Janoski is the matriarch of a family that has been growing and selling plants for generations at Janoski's Farm and Greenhouse in Clinton, Pa. When she caught wind of this book being written, JoAnn had the idea to create a Steel City Garden in her own backyard.

JoAnn's gardens are planted around the house, which stands next to the Farm Market and Greenhouse. It's situated in front of acres of farmland along Route 30.

Every season, JoAnn and her "helper" Jinny Pfeiffer make the short walk to the greenhouse to decide what's going to be planted where. The two stroll down long aisles filled with flowers, finding just the right combinations.

"Jinny is the biggest Steelers fan," JoAnn says. "I always let her do what she wants in the back garden."

And that's just where this black and gold garden is planted. It's filled with black-eyed Susan vine, 'Mystic Illusion' dahlias, 'Phantom' petunias, pretty yellow bidens, and more.

"Yellow is my favorite color," says Jinny. "Those bidens are a pretty hardy plant and are easy to grow." To prepare the soil for planting, she amends it with mushroom compost, maybe some top soil and/or peat moss. She also digs in a good granular fertilizer. During the season, she uses a liquid fertilizer every 10 days to keep the plants happy.

This garden isn't for the public, it's Jinny and JoAnn's, and both have found joy in the black and gold, especially Jinny ("I love the Steelers!"). This garden is a tribute to her favorite team.

Jinny thinks anyone could plant a Steel City Garden; it's just about finding the right plants for the right place. "It looks beautiful this year," she says, "We're really happy with it."

Butterflies, Bees & Garden Décor

Tip This is a project the whole family can have fun with.

My daughter, Stephanie, created it, but I helped a little. Our birdhouse project started when a friend was cleaning out her house and had 10 old birdhouses to get rid of. I gladly took them and painted each one with a white base coat.

Steph begged me to make an art project out of them. So we went to the local craft store (Michael's), bought some acrylic paints – "bling," as my daughter calls it – and went about the business of setting her up to start work on the birdhouses. I put an old sheet over a table outside and let her loose without instructions.

It can be hard for parents to let their kids just create; it's hard to know what they will come up with. It doesn't matter if it's good or bad, the creative process has been unleashed. In this case, the results were amazing. Each birdhouse was painted and decorated differently, with a rainbow of colors, bling installed; I loved her hand prints pressed on each side of the bigger ones.

That fall, we fastened the birdhouses to trees in the woods, on posts in the garden and hung some around our home. As spring unfolded, the birds discovered them and we watched together as black-capped chickadees, titmice and house wrens nested. Some raised their young and didn't return; others came back for a second generation.

This summer, Steph wanted to make a black and gold birdhouse in honor of her favorite team, the Penguins. I painted the birdhouse with the basic colors and she went to work again with the bling, and of course proudly added her signature handprints to each side.

I attached it to a tree along one of our main woodland paths, and now we can't wait to see what nests in the box next spring.

A goldfinch would be perfect!

SWALLOWTAIL BUTTERFLY
Papilio glaucus

 Tip How do you know if the caterpillar you see in your garden is going to one day become a swallowtail butterfly? The swallowtail caterpillars are two inches long and have alternating black and yellow spotted bands around leaf-green bodies.

One of the reasons we don't use chemicals in the garden is to keep pollinators like the Eastern Tiger Swallowtail Butterfly safe.

This butterfly variety has the colors we're looking for in our black and gold garden.

Many of the plants in this book will attract butterflies. There are a few things you can do in the garden to make it butterfly friendly. First and foremost is to eliminate the use of chemical pesticides and herbicides. There's no reason to use them, since there's an organic choice for just about any garden problem. I like to say that organic and chemical gardeners share the same problems, but use different solutions.

To attract and keep butterflies, grow a wide variety of plants known to be a food source for them. Many times the larvae (caterpillars) will feed on different plants than the adults who are looking for nectar.

Sunflowers, zinnias, butterfly bushes and marigolds are just some of the plants they will seek out.

Butterflies will congregate in wet, muddy puddles. Help them out and create a few in the garden. A shallow water dish will also attract them.

Here's what you can do: Learn which butterflies are common in your area, then figure out what their favorite host plants are. A butterfly garden should be out in the sun – the butterflies like that. But they also enjoy a shady place to cool off during the hottest part of the day.

They are attracted by color. Put lots of colorful sun-loving plants together in an attempt to bring in as many butterflies as possible. Diversity is the key; pick lots of different plants that will bloom from frost to frost.

One of the most wonderful things to do in the garden is sit and watch the butterflies enjoying the flowers.

CONTAINER CLEATS
Runnius fastius

- 🌸 Short lived perennial shoes
- 🌸 Full sun

 Tip If you like the sports theme of the cleats, try an old black baseball glove for a container. The leather will last for years and the webbing of the pocket will allow good drainage.

Have fun in the garden! That's my motto. I love to turn all sorts of things into containers. The trick is to find the right plant for the right container. So, what works in a pair of old cleats?

There are two plants I like to use in this situation: portulaca and sedum. As you can see from the photo, these black cleats and beautiful yellow portulaca are the perfect fit for the Steel City Garden. Size 12 will need less watering than size 7½.

Fill the shoe with a good planting mix and then push the roots of the plant down into the shoe. I like to soak the shoes in water for a few hours after planting; this gets the plants off to a good start.

My garden is filled with old boots and shoes planted with different succulents. My wife won't let me put those containers in front of the house. I can live with that.

WHERE IT WORKS BEST

Full sun is always best for these plants, but the containers (shoes) are so small, they will dry out quickly. I'd put them in morning sun with late afternoon shade. Since portulaca and sedum are bulletproof, they will only need to be watered every couple of days.

Give them some liquid organic fertilizer every few weeks.

PESTS AND DISEASES

Both plants are pest and disease free.

PLANT PARTNERS

None needed.

THE PERFECT CONTAINER
'Phantom' Petunia, *Osteospermum* 'Golden Serenity,'
Bidens 'Goldilocks Rocks'

✿ Annual
  bedding
  plants

✿ Full sun

 Tip There's a saying for containers: "Plant a thriller, filler and spiller." The thriller is the show-stopper in the middle, surrounded by the filler, and then the spiller hangs over the edges of the pot.

This is an example of the perfect black and gold container. I talk about all three of these plants in the book, and they are magic together. But many of the plants highlighted on these pages can be grouped together to beautiful effect in containers. Or even a single yellow variety in a black container. What can possibly go wrong... it's black and gold!

I saw this pot at Janoski's Farm and Greenhouse in Clinton, Pa., and had to have it – an especially nice touch to enhance our theme. I've had it on my outdoor dining table all summer and it's continued to bloom relentlessly.

When choosing a container, bigger is always better. And the more planting mix the better, so you won't need to water so often. Never use garden soil or heavy potting soil to fill a container. Choose an organic planting mix; it's lighter, drains well and is just better for the plants. Your plants will appreciate a feeding every couple of weeks with a good liquid organic fertilizer.

WHERE IT WORKS BEST

The great thing about growing in containers is they can be moved to add instant color anywhere in the garden. Eight hours of sun, beginning in the morning, will keep them thriving.

Containers are a great idea in the spring when rain is plentiful. But a dry summer might have you re-thinking growing in pots, as they might need water every other day. Containers need constant moisture and regular feeding to keep them growing strong.

PESTS AND DISEASES

Aphids, mealybugs, spider mites, thrips and fungal diseases affect many flowers.

Aphids, mealybugs, spider mites and thrips: Control with insecticidal soap or horticultural oil.

Fungal issues: Treat with an organic fungicide.

PLANT PARTNERS

None needed.

BLACK & GOLD FLAMINGOS
Phoenicopterus pittsburghius

- ❀ Plastic decorative birds
- ❀ Full sun to full shade

Tip Add a pair every year to eventually form a flock. The neighbors will love you.

These rare-colored birds might be considered ugly ducklings wading through the shallows of a Florida wetland next to garish pink flamingos, but no black and gold garden is complete without them.

The majestic birds were first discovered among the banners and flags of the Mike Feinberg Company in Pittsburgh's Strip District. If you bring them home, they will let visitors know you not only have good taste, but a keen design sense in the garden.

Oh, some might call them tacky, but we know better.

Make a bold statement in the garden with black and gold flamingos. One of the most surprising things about having them in my garden is that they attract the wild black and gold flamingos who will land to take a break on their migrating flight from Iowa to the North Shore of Pittsburgh.

WHERE IT WORKS BEST

There's only one place for these and that's the front yard next to a gazing ball.

PESTS AND DISEASES

No serious pests or diseases.

PLANT PARTNERS

Black-eyed Susan

EUROPEAN HONEYBEE
Apis mellifera

 Tip A hive has a range of a few miles, so if you hear of someone including one in their garden, don't resist, rejoice!

Honeybees are in trouble and gardeners can help them. Colony Collapse Disorder, mites and environmental issues have one of our most important pollinators on the run.

There's a fascinating documentary from PBS that shows a town in China where the bees have been wiped out by overuse of pesticides. The main crop for that area is pears. Without bees, each pear blossom needs to be hand pollinated and then covered with a translucent fabric. Can you imagine how many people are needed to pollinate an orchard?

Anyone who knows me knows what I'm going to say next: Don't use those pesticides and herbicides in your garden.

I don't spray anything in my garden because I don't have to. The good bugs eat the bad bugs. Nature creates a pretty good balance when we don't spray. If a problem arises, diagnose it and specifically target the pest or disease with an organic control.

Don't fear honeybees. They are workers relentlessly searching for food. The only time they will bother you is during an accidental encounter. As a kid, I ran barefoot over the clover lawns planted after World War II. A couple of times during the summer, I'd step on a honeybee. Now I'm *keeping* honeybees.

I'd fantasized for years about being a beekeeper and finally brought a hive into the garden in 2010. It sits in the corner of the vegetable garden and I can count on one hand how many times I've been stung. It's usually a chance encounter at the wrong time and wrong place.

There are many reasons to help the bees. First is the pollination. I've never seen so many cucumbers and other vine crops in my garden. Second is the honey. When looking for some, get the local stuff. It hasn't been pasteurized and had all the good stuff cooked out of it.

Local honey should be easy to find these days and has many wonderful properties for us. There is nothing like local honey. Think of it in the same way you regard a home-grown tomato.

    The stunning combination of black-eyed Susans against a 'Black Lace' elderberry greets visitors to the front yard of Andy Weigel's Steel City Garden. He lives on a quiet little street in Munhall, Pa., with his wife, Julie, and daughter, Leona. He came to Pittsburgh for a job 10 years ago and has lived in this home since 2010.

    Andy grew up right in the mid-section of Pennsylvania, where half of the sports fans root for East Coast teams and the other half are into Pittsburgh franchises. From an early age he fell in love with the Pirates, and specifically Andy Van Slyke, because they shared first names.

He has created a wonderful Black and Gold garden with the help of his father, George, who is a garden writer and amazing garden designer.

"It's just something neat to do in the garden," Andy said with a smile, referring to the color scheme. Andy and his dad sat down together to figure out which plants would work for the landscape. What they came up with looks great. Besides the black-eyed Susans and 'Black Lace' elderberry, he's also growing beautiful variegated black peppers, 'Mellow Yellow' spirea, black mondo grass, Shasta daisies, a fringe tree, yellow mums and more.

They wanted to revamp the "awful" landscaping inherited when the family moved in and "we figured black and gold would be easy," Andy said. At least that's what father and son thought when they created the plan.

"Surprisingly, we had to go to just about every nursery within 50 miles to find everything," Andy said, laughing. Don't worry though, depending on what you're looking for, gardeners will be able to find many choices for their Steel City Garden.

Sitting on his front porch, looking over the garden, he explained what it is about the garden that inspired him to care for this special landscape. "It's just a sense of community, keeping the neighborhood looking nice – and it keeps me out of trouble too."

ACKNOWLEDGMENTS

Thanks to my wife, Cindy, who always inspires me with a smile – which comes so easily. Thank you, Tim, Matt and Stephanie, for being so understanding of my work schedule and sharing time with me whether it's 1 p.m. or 1 a.m.

This book could never have been completed without the help of the nurseries, gardeners, gardens and garden businesses who let me photograph their plants or loaned me pictures of the varieties I couldn't find locally. Thank you to Hahn Nursery, Soergel Orchards, Janoski's Farm and Greenhouse, Best Feeds Garden Center, Phipps Conservatory and Botanical Gardens. To Jere Gettle at Baker Creek Heirloom Seeds, for allowing me to use so many pictures from your wonderful catalog. To my friends at Renee's Garden, Gardener's Supply, and Dramm, for all the help in finding the right tools and seeds for *The Steel City Garden*.

Thank you, Diana and Bill Knapp, for opening your amazing garden so I could get last-minute photos for this book.

Thank you to Bernie Pintar for telling me about your black and gold garden. To George Weigel for introducing me to your son, Andy Weigel, and for helping him create an awesome Steel City Garden. And thank you, Jinny Pfeiffer and JoAnn Janoski, for sharing your beautiful garden with readers.

To Pat Stone at Greenprints for sharing the wonderful Kathy Chapman story and cool artwork from Matt Collins.

To my best friend from fifth grade, Ed Kornuc, and your wife, Gail, for letting me stay at your estate Blorngornington and photograph your beautiful garden.

Thanks to Pam Panchak for taking pictures of me and making me look as good as possible (no easy feat).

To my publisher, Paul Kelly, for again coming up with a great idea for a book. To Cathy Dees, for turning my words into something readable, and Holly Rosborough, for designing a beautiful book.

And a special thank you to Gern Blanston, who has provided constant inspiration since we first connected back in the late 1970s.

WITH APPRECIATION FOR THE SUPPORT OF THESE PEOPLE, PLACES AND BUSINESSES

Baker Creek Heirloom Seed Co.
2278 Baker Creek Road
Mansfield, MO 65704
(417) 924-8917
seeds@rareseeds.com
www.rareseeds.com

Dramm
2000 North 18th Street
Manitowoc, WI 54220
(920) 684-0227
garden@dramm.com
www.dramm.com

Gardener's Supply Co.
128 Intervale Road
Burlington, VT 05401
1-800-876-5520
www.gardeners.com

Renee's Garden
6060 Graham Hill Road
Felton, CA 95018
1-888-880-7228
customerservice@reneesgarden.com
www.reneesgarden.com

Many of the plants were photographed at the places below:

Best Feeds Garden Center
2105 Babcock Boulevard
Pittsburgh, PA 15209
(412) 822-7777
www.bestfeedsgardencenters.com

Hahn Nursery Garden Center
5443 Babcock Boulevard
Pittsburgh, PA 15237
(412) 635-7475
www.facebook.com/Hahn.Nursery

Janoski's Farm and Greenhouse
1714 State Route 30
Clinton, PA 15026
(724) 899-3438
info@janoskis.com
www.janoskis.com

**Phipps Conservatory and
Botanical Gardens**
1 Schenley Park
Pittsburgh, PA 15213
(412) 622-6914
www.phipps.conservatory.org

Soergel Orchards
2573 Brandt School Road
Wexford, PA 15090
(724) 935-2090
folks@soergels.com
www.soergels.com

**Blorngornington, the estate
of Edward Kornuc**

My garden at Rosshaven

INDEX

ABOUT THE AUTHOR

Since moving to Pittsburgh in 1998, Doug has adopted the city as his home town and loves living there. But old habits die hard; as a northeastern Ohio native, he would never betray his beloved Browns by rooting for another team. His wife, Cindy, however, who was also born near Cleveland, enthusiastically roots for her adopted black and gold teams.

Doug is the Pittsburgh Post-Gazette's Backyard Gardener and co-host of the popular Sunday morning radio show "The Organic Gardeners" on KDKA radio. He's also an Emmy-award winner for the PBS documentary, "The Gardens of Pennsylvania." Doug created, wrote, produced and starred in the show, which was made at WQED-TV in Pittsburgh (but it was Cindy's idea). Doug has won many national awards from the Garden Writers Association, and he's been awarded Best Talent twice for his weekly "Digging with Doug" video series for the Post-Gazette.

He and Cindy live on four acres just north of Pittsburgh. They have three grown children. "The garden is the place our family always gathers," he says. "When my kids visit for dinner, they always want the fresh organic produce they grew up with, because nothing can compare."

The Steel City Garden is Doug's fifth title with St. Lynn's Press. *Tomatoes Garlic Basil,* his most recent book, was inspired by a trip he and Cindy took to Italy for their 25th anniversary, which was a chance for his wife to discover and explore her Italian grandmother's home town.

Doug loves to hear from other gardeners. If you have an interesting garden story or just want to say "Hi," drop him a line. Doug hopes you remember the most important piece of advice he can offer: "Gardening is fun."

www.dougoster.com • www.steelcitygarden.com • www.facebook.com/doug.oster.garden
Twitter@dougoster1 • dougoster@comcast.net

Doug Oster • P.O. Box 11013 • Pittsburgh, PA 15237